John Kaag

SICK SOULS, HEALTHY MINDS

John Kaag is the author of *American Philosophy: A Love Story*, which was named a *New York Times* Editors' Choice and an NPR Best Book of the year, and *Hiking with Nietzsche: On Becoming Who You Are*, which was also an NPR Best Book of the year. His writing has appeared in the *New York Times*, *Harper's Magazine*, and many other publications. He is professor of philosophy at the University of Massachusetts, Lowell, and lives in Carlisle, Massachusetts. Twitter @JohnKaag

Sick Souls, Healthy Minds

Sick Souls, Healthy Minds

How William James Can Save Your Life

John Kaag

PRINCETON UNIVERSITY PRESS

PRINCETON AND OXFORD

Requests for permission to reproduce material from this work
should be sent to permissions@press.princeton.edu

Published by Princeton University Press
41 William Street, Princeton, New Jersey 08540
6 Oxford Street, Woodstock, Oxfordshire OX20 1TR

press.princeton.edu

ISBN 9780691192161
ISBN (e-book) 9780691200934

British Library Cataloging-in-Publication Data is available

Editorial: Rob Tempio and Matt Rohal
Production Editorial: Natalie Baan
Text Design: Leslie Flis
Cover Design: Jason Anscomb
Production: Erin Suydam
Publicity: Katie Lewis and Maria Whelan
Copyeditor: Hank Southgate

Cover Credit: William James, *Here I and Sorrow Sit*, red-crayon
drawing. MS Am 1092.2 (54), Houghton Library, Harvard University

Versions of these chapters have been excerpted in slightly altered
form in the *Chronicle of Higher Education*, *Aeon Magazine*, and
The Towner Magazine.

This book has been composed in Sabon LT Std

Printed on acid-free paper. ∞

Printed in the United States of America

10 9 8 7 6 5 4 3 2 1

For Doug Anderson and for Kathy

Contents

Prologue: "A Disgust for Life"   1

1   Determinism and Despair   11

2   Freedom and Life   42

3   Psychology and the Healthy Mind   68

4   Consciousness and Transcendence   94

5   Truth and Consequences   126

6   Wonder and Hope   169

Acknowledgments   185

Notes   187

Suggested Reading   197

Index   201

Sick Souls, Healthy Minds

Prologue

"A DISGUST FOR LIFE"

Take the happiest man, the one most envied
by the world, and in nine cases out of ten his
inmost consciousness is one of failure.
—William James, *The Varieties of
Religious Experience*, 1903

"I AM A LOW-LIVED WRETCH. I've been prey to such disgust for life during the past three months as to make letter writing almost an impossibility." William James was on the brink of adulthood and, as he confessed to his friend Henry Bowditch in 1869, on the brink of collapse. In the coming two decades, James would write—letters, essays, books—incessantly, like his life depended on it. He'd become the father of American philosophy and psychology, but when he wrote to Bowditch he couldn't foresee any of it. Actually, he often struggled to see the next day.[1]

James had just returned to his father's house in Cambridge, Massachusetts, after an eighteen-month sojourn in Berlin. This trip, a quest in search of good health and sanity, had failed. More accurately, it had proven deeply counterproductive. He was, if anything, deeper in the pit. Back in New England, the prospect of earning his medical degree—which he'd go on to do without difficulty—gave him little joy. His heart wasn't in it, wasn't in anything. In truth, it may have been in too many things at once.

James's polymathic abilities were, partially, responsible for his divided self—part poet, part biologist, part artist, part mystic. He was pulled in too many directions, like a man on the rack, and therefore, for a time, couldn't move, forward or otherwise. He was a man of disparate pieces, and in his early years he nearly failed to hold himself together. But there was something else. James was also philosophically stuck, mired in thoughts that had plagued countless thinkers before him: maybe human beings are determined by forces beyond their control; maybe their lives are destined from the start, fated to end tragically and meaninglessly; maybe human beings, despite their best efforts, can't act on their own behalf, as free and vibrant beings; maybe they're nothing but cogs in an unfortunately constructed machine.

Meaninglessness was the problem, James's problem, and it drove him to the edge of suicide. In the late 1860s, he used a red crayon to sketch a portrait in a notebook: a young man sitting alone, shoulders hunched, head down. Over the figure James wrote,

"HERE I AND SORROW SIT." But if you look closely, very closely, you will see a faint line that makes all the difference. Read it again: the "N" might actually be an "M." It says, "HERE I AM." This was a self-portrait.[2]

In his later life, James described an individual, all too common to the neighborhood around Harvard, who is, from birth, psychologically vexed: "There are persons whose existence is little more than a series of zigzags, as now one tendency and now another gets the upper hand. Their spirit wars with their flesh, they wish for incompatibles, wayward impulses interrupt their most deliberate plans, and their lives are one long drama of repentance and of effort to repair misdemeanors and mistakes."[3] These are, in James's words, the "sick-souled," those who were just as likely to graduate from the Ivy League as to commit suicide at McLean Asylum, a stone's throw from Harvard Yard. Rumors have swirled for more than a century that James had his own stint at the hospital, but they have faded in the hundred years after his death. Today, James is usually described as a man who faced mental illness without the help of doctors.

This isn't exactly true: he *was* the doctor. William James's entire philosophy, from beginning to end, was geared to save a life, *his* life.[4] Philosophy was never a detached intellectual exercise or a matter of wordplay. It wasn't a game, or if it was, it was the world's most serious. It was about being thoughtful and living vibrantly. I would like to offer the reader James's existential life preserver. Of course, in the end, life is a terminal condition. No one makes it out alive. But some authors—James most notably—can help us survive, so to speak, by preserving and passing on what is most important about being human before we pass away. James crafted what he called a philosophy of healthy-mindedness. It may not be a formal antidote for the sick soul, but I like to think of it as an effective home remedy.

Such a philosophy would be wholly unnecessary were it not for the fact that so many of us seem to teeter on the brink of the abyss. In 2010, I was there myself. I was thirty, in the midst of a divorce, and had just watched my estranged, alcoholic father die. And I was at Harvard on a postdoc writing about—you guessed it—William James. I was supposed to be finishing a monograph about his notion of creativity, an uplifting book about the salvific effects of his philosophy known as pragmatism. Pragmatism, James informed his readers in 1900, holds that truth should be judged on its practical consequences, on the way that it impacts life. It's a nice thought, except when life itself seems pretty meaningless. James knew this and crafted a philosophy to address this painful insight. It took me several miserable years to grasp it.

I think William James's philosophy saved my life. Or, more accurately, it encouraged me not to be afraid of life. This is not to say it will work for everyone. Hell, it's not even to say that it will work for me tomorrow. Or that it works all the time. But it did happen, at least once, and that is enough to make me eternally grateful and more than a little hopeful about the prospects of this book. James wrote for our age: one that eschews tradition and superstition but desperately craves existential meaning; one that is defined by affluence but also depression and acute anxiety; one that valorizes icons who ultimately decide that the life of fame is one that really ought to be cut short prematurely. To such a culture, James gently, persistently urges, "Be not afraid of life. Believe that life is worth living, and your belief will help create the fact."[5] On good days, when my own sick soul speaks only quietly, James's insistence works very well. On bad days, it helps me hang on. As I've come to admire and cherish James's philosophy as a lifesaver, I've also encountered a growing number of friends, neighbors, students, and strangers who flounder in the profoundest ways possible.

In 2014, I rode my bike to Harvard University, to Widener Library, to finally finish that uplifting book on James's pragmatism. I was doing better—the book now seemed possible, even somewhat realistic. It was a frigid, snow-covered February morning. I don't know what possessed me to ride my bike, but ride I did, slipping and sliding my way from Charlestown into Cambridge. The last leg of my ride was along Kirkland Avenue, in front of William James Hall, but on that day the road around the massive building was cordoned off in yellow police tape.

William James Hall dwarfs the classical buildings that surround it. Most of Harvard was constructed with a mind to Puritan propriety, set out horizontally in accord with the belief that the heavens should be left for God. This building, however, was not erected in the spirit of this humility. Built in 1963 by Minoru Yamasaki—the designer of the World Trade Center—the skyscraper, which today houses the Department of Psychology, is pointedly modern. Monumental and humorless, it stands as a serious tribute to a man who was arguably the greatest of Harvard's great minds.

From the roof of William James Hall, you could throw a rock and hit James's onetime home on 95 Irving Street. As it was constructed in 1889, James called his house "Elysium": heaven looked like a three-story, gambrel-roofed Colonial revival, with a spacious library on the first floor and an intimate study on the second. Pitch a stone in the opposite direction from William James Hall, and you would just miss Emerson Hall, in Harvard Yard, where James, in the first years of the twentieth century, founded a uniquely American brand of philosophy. Ralph Waldo Emerson, James's intellectual godparent, had heralded the coming of a new type of thinker in 1837, in "The American Scholar," who would go on to put the nation on the intellectual map. When James died in 1910, at the age of sixty-eight, he had done his very best to fulfill Emerson's prophecy.

The fifteenth floor of William James Hall is one of the few saving graces of this monstrous building. In its central seminar room hangs a portrait of James in three-quarter view, looking out a window, his deep-set, piercing eyes cast off the edge of the canvas, down across the university that he helped make famous. The view from the fifteenth floor is spectacular, and its balcony, at 170 feet, provides a fresh vantage point of James's surroundings.

At 170 feet, it takes a human body a little less than four seconds to hit the ground at seventy miles per hour. The last time that happened was on the icy morning of February 6, 2014. A 2006 Harvard alumnus, Steven Rose, at the age of twenty-nine, took his life by jumping from the roof of William James Hall, joining the more than forty thousand people who killed themselves that year. A professor who worked in the building reported that "we found it hard to go about our daily routines."[6]

The professor was right. I did not go about my "daily routine" that morning. In truth, I am pretty sure that events like these are supposed to interrupt one's daily grind. In the police blotter the next day, Rose's fall was described as "an unattended death," but I can assure you that this isn't exactly true. I dismounted my bike and joined several dozen onlookers at the perimeter of the restricted area on Kirkland to speculate what had happened. After standing in the cold for half an hour, most of us decided that the proper question was not "What had happened?" but rather "*Why* did it happen?"

It remains a very good question, one that defies a general or catchall answer. Until that point I had often thought that in my next life, I'd like to come back as a Harvard freshman. The opportunity and privilege—the sheer freedom of the experience—is unmatched and appears, from the outside, as an unqualified good. Of course, Steven Rose would probably tell me I was being stupid and insensitive. So would William James. There is no such thing as an unqualified good. Appearances can be deceiving. Freedom is often shot through with anxiety. Privilege can be an unshakable burden. And opportunity is easily squandered. It all depends on the particular life that is being led.

"Is life worth living?" In 1895, twenty-five years after contemplating suicide, James still wrestled with the question. According to James, there was exactly one answer that tracks the reality of Rose's death, but also might have saved his life: "Maybe." Maybe life is worth living—"it depends on the liver."[7] Maybe certain lives are so impossible or unbearable that they are better off cut short. Maybe Steven Rose's was one of them. But maybe not, James would suggest. Maybe there was still time to make good on the meaning of life, to find, but more likely to make, something of value before it was too late.

After an hour in the snow, the crowd dispersed, and by late afternoon the police tape had been removed from William James Hall. I did not go about my daily routine that day; instead I decided to write a book that James might have written for men and women like Steven Rose, a book that explores the "maybe" of life's worth, and, for the time being, decides that it is worth enough.

This is an attempt to pass James's wisdom on, to pass on his sense that life's possibilities are real, and can be explored freely, meaningfully, but only at our own risk. James came close to foreclosing these possibilities altogether as a young man. In the end, however, he suggested—in many different valences—that this is decidedly the wrong way to exit life. We all will spin off this mortal coil soon enough. The task is to find a way to live, truly live, in the interim. William James can help people find their way.

1

Determinism and Despair

The normal process of life contains moments
as bad as any of those which insane melancholy is filled with, moments in which radical
evil gets its innings and takes its solid turn.
The lunatic's visions of horror are all drawn
from the material of daily fact.

—William James, *The Varieties of*
Religious Experience, 1903

In a certain sense, the way that we take in life is
determined without our permission. No one asks us
if we would like to be born or if we might like to grow
up in this family rather than that one. One's race, sex,
socioeconomic condition, and health are factors that
are largely accidental. We are, in the words of the
twentieth-century German philosopher Martin Heidegger, "thrown" into the world, set adrift, and,
through much of adolescence, live at the mercy of
forces beyond our control.

For many people, adulthood does not free them from these circumstances. "Despite preconceptions that suicide is more prevalent in high-income countries," the World Health Organization states, "in reality, 75 percent of suicides [worldwide] occur in low- and middle-income countries." This statistic is, I assume, a function of being delivered into an intolerable situation and, in the end, refusing to tolerate it. Of course, if fate smiles upon us, the forces are benign and we are not born into abject poverty, but even the most benign forces can eventually cause one to flounder.[1]

William James, ostensibly, was a very lucky one. Born in 1842 in New York City, James grew up in a household supported by old money—lots of it—with a father, Henry James Sr., who doted on his children. James was indulged, but not in the ways we usually expect.

In 1832, Henry Sr. had inherited the better part of a million dollars, a vast sum in those days, from his father who had headed a banking and real estate empire in upstate New York. Henry Sr., however, was not going to go into the family business in Albany. Not even close. Now that he was independently wealthy, Henry turned away from worldly pursuits altogether, dedicating himself to the study of religion, philosophy, and the natural sciences.

When his eldest son, William, was born, Henry Sr. was in the midst of making his final break with the modern, materialistic rat race, but also with his own father's strict Calvinism that had kept everything in frantic motion. Calvinism, you see, is a religion of obedience and absolute control, God's control. Humans are either blessed, and therefore "elected" to heaven, or cursed, and therefore damned to hell. But there's no tried-and-true way of knowing what type of person you are. One thing is certain, however: you aren't in control of your destiny. In 1844, when William was two, Henry Sr. explained:

> I had . . . been in the habit of ascribing to the Creator, so far as my life and actions are concerned, an outside discernment of the most jealous scrutiny, and had accordingly put the greatest possible alertness into his service and worship, until my will, as you have seen— thoroughly fagged out as it were with the formal, endless, heartless task of conciliating a stony-hearted Deity—actually collapsed.[2]

For James the elder, Calvinism set out an impossible task: to exercise the human will freely, meaningfully, in order to satisfy a God who was both omnipotent and infinitely removed. Pursuing this task led Henry Sr. into what he would later term a "vastation," from the Latin *vastare*, meaning "to lay to waste"—a state of

utter spiritual and personal desolation. One was supposed to act as though one's actions mattered in some
moral and existential sense, but the conditions of
God's divine design suggested that they amounted to
pitifully little. God might have a plan, but the evils of
human existence remain.

Henry eventually escaped his "vastation" through
the mystical training of an eighteenth-century Lu-
theran mystic named Emanuel Swedenborg. In reading Swedenborg, Henry achieved an "emancipated
condition" and his spirit was "lifted by a sudden miracle into felt harmony with universal . . . and inde-
structible life."[3] The religious crisis that Henry James
experienced in the early 1840s set the rules of engage-
ment for the household in which William James would
be raised. Freedom: that was the enduring touchstone
that guided family life. William, along with his pre-
cocious brother and sister, Henry and Alice, were given
free rein to play, study, read, travel—do whatever—
as they liked. The only thing that was not permitted
was limiting these brilliant children's possibilities.
Even Wilkinson and Robertson, the two James brothers
whom their father did not single out for intellectual
greatness, were given a generous leash.

There was some method, even a beautiful one,
behind the father's madness. He believed that the
point of life wasn't merely to make a living, to assume

some narrowly circumscribed task and do it repeatedly day after day. It wasn't about making money or punching a clock. Instead, the objective of human existence was to cultivate good character. "And in as much," Henry Sr. wrote of raising a son, "as I know that this character cannot be forcibly imposed on him, but must be freely assumed, I surround him as far as possible with an atmosphere of freedom."[4]

William James grew up, as one might expect of a boy charged with the task of being free, on the move: Paris, Rouen, Kent, and London by the age of two; Albany at four; New York City at five. In 1855, his father concluded that the educational system of the New York elite was far too constrictive for a ten-year-old, so off the family went again: back to Paris, then on to Lyon, Geneva, and finally to Boulogne-sur-Mer on the French side of the English Channel.

Ralph Waldo Emerson, one of Henry James Sr.'s closest friends, suggested that "traveling is a fool's paradise," but it worked rather well in the upbringing of William James, at least for a time. His father hoped that his children would simply "be somewhere—almost anywhere would do—and somehow receive an impression or an accession, feel a relation or vibration."[5] That was enough. James's formal education was anything but formal, a by-product of happenstance, or better, exposure—James was exposed to the world, encouraged to experience its riches often and its deficiencies occasionally, and to experiment with its natural and cultural offerings. In truth, his father hoped that his son would experiment with himself—hypothesize, test, and observe what a young man might become.

When the teenaged James dedicated himself to one experiment at the expense of others, however, his father was quick to warn him against narrowing his scope prematurely. This seems to have been the case in 1860 when the James family uprooted again, traveling to Newport, Rhode Island, so William could study painting with William Hunt, arguably the most talented American portraitist of the day. Henry Sr. initially supported his son's enthusiasm, but reminded him that this vocation, even such a pointedly unconventional one, could have the effect of stifling his personal growth. Despite the freewheeling atmosphere of his childhood, William's father had still always known best, but on this occasion met with resistance: "I do not see why man's spiritual culture," William wrote to his father in August of 1860, "should not go on independently of his aesthetic activity, why the power an artist feels in himself should tempt him to forget what he is, any more than the power felt by Cuvier or Fourier would tempt them to do the same."[6]

Despite this protest, James's foray into professional painting lasted but a year. Did he discover that his sense of perfectionism outstripped his technical artistic skill? Probably. Did his father's disapproval also wear down his resolve? Definitely. In any event, in 1861 James left Newport, assuming an intellectual bearing that he would keep, more or less consistently, for the rest of his life: William James was bound for science. His comment regarding Cuvier and Fourier—the biologist and physicist par excellence—would be a harbinger of James's persistent attempt to join Asa Gray, Louis Agassiz, and Benjamin Peirce as an American man of science. Henry James Sr. was more satisfied with this course of action. *Scientia*—knowledge—would set his son free.

If this sounds like the opening pages of a story about a poor little rich boy, it is. At least it is in part. James was given every possible opportunity to flourish and be shielded from the world's harsher realities. He was, in the simplest possible terms, spoiled.

There are, however, reasons to forbear this story. James's pampered adolescence and subsequent disillusionment mirror, with disturbing fidelity, the psychic fracturing that has come to define many lives of contemporary privilege. I'm not just talking about the Kate Spades, Margot Kidders, and Anthony Bourdains of the world—although their suicides stand as dramatic and especially tragic recent cases—but rather anyone who has ever had enough free time on his or her hands to consider the possibility that life might actually be wholly meaningless. Thomas Hobbes might be right that leisure is the mother of philosophy, but leisure also, for many people, spawns morbid depression. It is as if only after a person has been given everything that one has the chance to realize that everything might never be enough to really matter. It only takes a minor disturbance in the comforts of daily life—just a persistent irritation in an otherwise perfect existence—to bring on this dark realization. At that point, in the words of the twentieth-century French thinker Albert Camus, "the stage sets collapse."[7] For William James, this began to occur in the spring of 1862.

This was the year in which William Morris Hunt, James's onetime painting instructor, painted *The Drummer Boy*. Against a darkening sky, a young boy, maybe ten years old, stands alone on a pedestal, alone save for the massive marching drum that he carries, his arm raised to the clouds ready to sound the call to arms. On the pedestal is a simple statement, an imperative for all able-bodied men: "U. S. Volunteers."

With the election of Abraham Lincoln, the Southern states had seceded, and the Civil War intensified.

Garth Wilkinson "Wilkie" James responded to the Drummer Boy's command immediately, enlisting in 1862 at the age of seventeen. "When I went to war I was a boy of 17 years of age, the son of parents devoted to the cause of the Union and the abolition of slavery," Wilkinson would later remember. "I had been brought up in the belief that slavery was a monstrous wrong, its destruction worthy of a man's best efforts, even unto the laying down of life."[8] He almost laid down his own in 1863 at the Battle of Fort Wagner, sustaining wounds from which he would never fully recover. Robertson James regarded his brother's injury as all the more reason to enter the fight in February of 1864.

But where was William James? He was of fighting age when the confrontation broke out, older than both his brothers. He too grew up in a household that abhorred slavery and enshrined the right to freedom. He too should have been willing to make the ultimate sacrifice for the Union cause. He might have been willing. But was he able? James never enlisted. He was his father's chosen boy, but also a rather sickly young man with bad eyesight. He stood on the sidelines as his younger brothers became real heroes, or, in the eyes of the nation, real men. Ralph Barton Perry,

James's student and his most charitable biographer, concludes, "I can see in William James no evidence whatever of his having entered manhood in the decade of the 1860s."[9]

Louis Menand argues that the Civil War set the context for James's philosophical studies: the devastation of a conflict, motivated by grand ideological visions, convinced James and his fellow pragmatists to fashion a philosophy of modest, testable beliefs and goals.[10] I tend to think that the Civil War affected James's outlook in a more immediate and jarring way. To watch relatively helplessly as loved ones go off to war, to witness the fragile inevitabilities of human existence, to experience impotence and stifled ambition—this was James's first intimation that he, along with the rest of the universe, was not free but rather fated.

Given the James family's near-obsession with liberty, William was almost destined to eventually feel himself thoroughly stuck. The young man's entire life had been premised on the expectation that he could exercise his free will. It was only a matter of time before he discovered that he couldn't. In the year before Wilkinson enlisted, James enrolled in Lawrence Scientific School, hoping to make his mark in chemistry, and then in physiology, but it could not have been without the sense that he was not man enough to make a *real* mark in the war that enveloped the nation. More than forty years later, James was still anxious to cultivate the martial spirit that he couldn't muster in his youth. In "The Moral Equivalent of War," delivered in 1906, James maintains that "militarism is the great preserver of our ideals of hardihood, and human life with no use for hardihood would be contemptible. Without risks or prizes for the darer, history would be insipid indeed."[11]

There were no meaningful "prizes for the darer" at Lawrence Scientific School. Here, James was drawn to what his teacher Charles William Eliot would call "unsystematic excursions"[12] in chemistry (James had always enjoyed ingesting the potions that he routinely made in his boyhood labs), but most of these experiments proved unfulfilling. They were, at best, a mere playing at the edges of the real world. And James, I think, knew it. Giving up chemistry, which he came to hate, and turning to biology, James began to feel the allure of what is left behind after meaning and passion run dry: money. "I feel very much the importance of making soon a final choice of my business in life," James admitted to his mother in November of 1863. Continuing, James wrote, "I stand now at the place where the road forks. One branch leads to material comfort, the fleshpots, but it seems kind of like selling one's soul. The other to mental dignity and independence; combined however with physical pen-ury." It was a decision between business, the life of the nine-to-five, and pure science, the life of knowledge. James would split the difference and try to become a doctor, but it was, I can only imagine, a half-hearted choice. The war continued to rage and James was not in it.[13]

Many people struggle with the decision of whether to sell their souls. They can get a good price, but the op-portunity costs seem awfully high. Awfully. James knew this. "The moral flabbiness born of the exclu-sive worship of the bitch-goddess SUCCESS. That— with the squalid cash interpretation put on the word 'success'—is our national disease," James wrote in later life.[14] The disease progresses so slowly and steadily, victims often don't even know they're sick. That is, until they reach the end of life and realize that they have been mortally ill for as long as they can re-member. At that point, there is no antidote, no cure, no respite. Just death. And regret.

Of course, it is very difficult to see the problem of working hard in order to live in the lap of luxury, in the "fleshpots" as James describes it. Everything seems so happily habitual and routine, comfortable even in the drudgery. Eventually, with any luck, you don't even have to toil. The money you once saved now actually makes more money. Everything is accomplished by way of a strange word called "interest." You don't even have to think about it. There is no problem with the fleshpots, save perhaps one. As James deliberated about his future, he was reading the works of the German philosopher Arthur Schopenhauer, who put his finger on it: "[I]f all wishes were fulfilled as soon as they arose, how would men occupy their lives? What would they do with their time? If the world were a paradise of luxury and ease, a land flowing with milk and honey, where every Jack obtained his Jill at once and without any difficulty, men would either die of boredom or hang themselves."[15] Schopenhauer suspected that in the absence of genuine hardship some individuals would fabricate it—they would pointedly seek out danger and discomfort—for no other reason than to escape ennui. James was one of them.

In 1865, James interrupted his medical studies to join Louis Agassiz's expedition to the Amazon. He wasn't healthy enough to fight, but he could still travel. Agassiz was one of James's teachers at Lawrence Scientific School and the preeminent zoologist and geologist in America. James's voyage to South America was made under the pretense of his interest in the biological sciences, but it scarcely masked the twenty-three-year-old's thrill seeking. This, however, might make the trip sound more superficial than it was. According to James, before the journey he said to himself, "W. J., in this excursion you will learn to know yourself and your resources somewhat more intimately than you do now, and will come back with your character considerably evolved and established."[16] This was meant to be a voyage of self-discovery, but like most trips of this sort James discovered more than he anticipated.

James was obviously looking for a bit of a challenge, something out of the ordinary. His student and friend Ella Lyman Cabot would later make the distinction between drudgery, which is simply monotony, and meaningful work, which involves attention, exertion, and experience. James was after meaningful work. He also, furtively, wanted to confront the existential terror that many men of his day had grappled with in war.

On his way to the Amazon, James wrote to his parents from Rio de Janeiro, rejoicing that "the horrors of this trip will [soon] be over." The description of the difficult voyage, however, was not without a sense of profound accomplishment: "O the vile sea! The damned Deep! No one has the right to write about the 'nature of Evil' or to have any opinion about evil, who has not been to sea." Really? His younger brother had been mowed down by cannon fire and nearly killed. He didn't have the right to write about evil? No, only the dilettante sailor has that right. James was now one of these rare hardy men. He'd met the sea in battle and won, writing that "the awful slough of despond into which you are there plunged furnishes too profound an experience not to be a fruitful one. I cannot say yet what the fruit is in my case, but I am sure some day an accession of wisdom from it."[17]

This was, at best, false bravado, the posturing of a young man who was trying to get ahold of himself. This is not unlike Goethe's Faust (one of James's favorite characters) craving the depths of experience, summoning the sublime Earth Spirit, and then promptly cowering before it. The world was simply too much for him. In the end, James was not robust enough to be an explorer: back pains, stomach flu, temporary blindness, anxiety, and depression forced him to truncate his adventure. The trip to Brazil, and James's mid-twenties on the whole, can be described as his recurrent failure to control his health and circumstances. His free will—the personal volition that had been preened and protected by his father—just wasn't up to the task.

Chronic illness, physical and psychological, is not unlike the sea. Seemingly limitless and unpredictable, completely indifferent to human plans and desires, there is little hope of counteracting it. And it takes a person down. Once under water, the very attempt to stay alive—the act of inhaling—hastens one's rapid demise. If James learned something on Agassiz's expedition, it was that human life, despite our best attempts to transcend our natural circumstance or brute animality, is governed, almost exclusively, by physical forces beyond our understanding and control.

In 1866, after returning to Boston and resuming medical school, James began a meticulous study of Marcus Aurelius, the Stoic. James only read two or three pages a day. The Stoic's message is, I will admit, somewhat difficult to digest. According to "Mark," as James fondly calls him, human beings consist of three parts: a "little flesh," "some breath," and something called "the ruling part." The first two of these are fragile and transitory: our body and breath come and go quickly, in a tragically disgusting fashion. At the end of the existential day, we are a bunch of meat sacks destined for the grinder. After confronting the force of the ocean and profound sickness, James knew this all too well. The "ruling part," however, sometimes translated as "reason," is the coping mechanism to deal with the tragedy of the human condition. The controlling part can face the nastiness of human finitude and bring our life into tune with any brutal reality. This isn't just a grin-and-bear-it philosophy, as Stoicism is often described, but rather an attempt to harmonize one's life with the cruel necessities of nature. As one becomes an adult, it is best to come to terms with gray hair, disease, and death. It's going to happen anyway.

In June of 1866, James wrote to his younger friend Thomas Ward, who recently had suffered from a bout of ill health. Urging him to take up Marcus Aurelius, James advises,

> It seems to me that any man who can, like him, grasp the love of a "life according to nature" i.e. a life in which your individual will becomes so harmonized to nature's will as cheerfully to acquiesce in whatever she assigns to you, know that you serve some purpose in her vast machinery which will never be revealed to you—any man who can do this will, I say, be a pleasing spectacle, no matter what his lot in life.[18]

In other words, everything can be stripped from a person except his or her free response to the horrible situation into which he or she has been thrown. That was the Stoic hope, one that James recommended to his friend Ward.

There was, however, a small problem with James becoming a Stoic. Stoicism was well fitted to the particular spiritual mind-set of Marcus Aurelius's Imperial Rome and also to Christianity, which arose in its wake. But it wasn't particularly suited to the perspective of modern science.

Stoicism turns on the presumption that there are two constitutive elements of every person: the bodily self that is subject to natural laws and the "ruling" spiritual self (a soul) that can determine its orientation to the workings of nature. While the bodily self is definitely not free, this "ruling part" is more or less at liberty to choose how to respond to its highly unfortunate circumstances. In the late 1860s, James came of age in an intellectual culture that began to question the religious framework that supported this dual vision of personhood. What if there were no such thing as a soul? What then of the "ruling part" that was so important to the Stoic?

As James extended his studies of the natural sciences, particularly biology and physiology, he began to encounter thinkers who held that human beings were a "little flesh" and "some breath"—but that was *all*. In that case, life was fully determined by nature and suffered as one long, senseless tragedy. This thought was the seed that ultimately grew into what James would later term the "dilemma of determinism." For James, in the late 1860s, it became a life-threatening crisis.

The idea of determinism, generally speaking, arises in the following way. Imagine you are asked a seemingly innocuous question: "Do you believe in science?" James certainly did, so let's assume you do too. Now, if you believe in science, you probably also believe in causation, the principle that the events and occurrences in the world can be traced to certain causes that bring them about. There are rational but also very personal reasons to grant causation. The principle allows people to make sense of the change they see in the world, but also to hold that their actions can effect some change.

If you don't accept causation—the basics of cause and effect—you are basically saying that the universe is just a chaotic mess. So let's say you endorse some form of causation. And just for the sake of argument, let's assume you also accept a very basic philosophical position called the "principle of sufficient reason," which states that everything that exists has a reason for being and being as it is, and not otherwise. That makes pretty good sense, right? It just means that *in principle* everything can be explained in terms of its causes.

We can see the principle of sufficient reason at work in our understanding of the natural world in a fairly obvious and uncontroversial way. If we want to know how the vessels in Agassiz's expedition reached Brazil, we can give a very detailed description of fluid dynamics, propulsion, wind currents, water currents, and the like to explain their movement—how they went from here to there governed by certain natural laws. Natural objects don't just have one or two causes, but rather an indefinite series of causes that account for their existence and position in the world.

Follow this train of thought far enough and you'll arrive at determinism, which holds that given the state of affairs at any point in time, the way things go thereafter is determined, or fixed, in accord with natural law. It has always been this way, and it always will be. James described the determinist's position in 1884:

> It professes that those parts of the universe already laid down absolutely appoint and decree what the other parts shall be. The future has no ambiguous possibilities hidden in its womb; the part we call the present is compatible with only one totality. Any other future complement than the one fixed from eternity is impossible. The whole is in each and every part, and welds it with the rest into an absolute unity, an iron block, in which there can be no equivocation or shadow of turning.[19]

At first glance, this might seem like a rather boring discussion in the history of Western philosophy. And for almost two millennia—from the rise of Christianity to 1800—it pretty much was. So things have causes? So what. Humans are different than things: they have souls and minds and free will and can do as they please. But then, in the 1860s, just as James ventured earnestly into philosophy, the terms of the discussion changed, and the debate surrounding determinism became very interesting and equally disturbing.

With the publication of Darwin's *Origin of Species* in 1859, a heretical idea gained significant traction in the philosophical communities of Europe and the United States: human beings were just animals— extremely smart animals maybe, but still just animals. Darwin avoided making this conclusion explicit, but it was, many theorists believed, a necessary implication of his theory of evolution. At the very least, in the wake of Darwin, one had to figure out what his theory meant and where it ultimately led. In 1911, James's friend and colleague Josiah Royce reflected that James had led a group of thinkers—what he called the "second generation" of evolutionary theorists—in extending and evaluating a genuinely new way to understand human nature.[20]

Thomas Huxley, the boldest of Darwin's defenders and an expert in comparative anatomy, published

Evidence as to Man's Place in Nature in 1863 and in it outlined the close relationship between human beings and apes. Previous generations of philosophers had the luxury of thinking that nonhuman animals might be fully controlled by the laws of nature but that humans were somehow different, somehow free. Huxley disabused his readers of this notion.

In 1865, the twenty-three-year-old William James published his first review in the *North American Review* on Huxley's *Lectures on the Elements of Comparative Anatomy*. James admired Huxley's courage in standing by the facts of science, lauding him for maintaining "the view of the phenomena of life (including human life) which makes them result from the general laws of matter, rather than from the subordination of those laws to some principle of individuality, different in each case." In other words, James couldn't argue with Huxley for believing that human beings, like other animals, were governed by natural law. Like Huxley, James supported the Darwinian hypothesis, but this didn't mean that James wasn't also terrified by its implications. Huxley's view, according to James, was "hypothetically at least, atheistic in its tendency, and, as such, its progress causes much alarm to many excellent people."[21] There was something, however, even more alarming for James: Huxley's materialism teetered on the edge of causal determinism and jeopardized free will. And this shook young James to the core. He had to figure out how human freedom could coincide with the findings of evolutionary theory, which seemed largely indisputable.

In the mid-1860s, James was easily shaken. He took another hiatus from medical school in 1867, but this time not with an eye to adventure seeking. James's health had declined dramatically, and now partial blindness, headaches, and nausea made studying impossible. Mysterious weakness of the back, what James called his "dorsal condition," often prevented the twenty-five-year-old from sitting upright or walking. He was immobile, stuck, incapacitated—thoroughly unfree.

With the blessing of his father, James left for Germany, with the peripheral intention of working in its famed physiology laboratories, but primarily in the hope that he would find some physical relief at the spas outside of Berlin. By September, however, James wrote to Henry James Sr. from Dresden that the water treatments of the area had been ineffectual: he was contemplating suicide, admitting, "the thoughts of the pistol, the dagger and the bowl began to usurp an unduly large part of my attention, and I began to think that some change, even if a hazardous one, was necessary."[22]

Better to change, even in dangerous and self-destructive ways, than to languish in inactivity. At least killing yourself was a definitive action—something James could actually *do*—compared to the doldrums of passivity. Schopenhauer lingered in the background of James's thoughts, reminding a reader, "They tell us that suicide is the greatest piece of cowardice . . . that suicide is wrong; when it is quite obvious that there is nothing in the world to which every man has a more unassailable title than to his own life and person."[23] Suicide can be regarded not as a letting go, but rather a laying claim to a life that is otherwise out of control. Control: that is what James wanted. He craved a sense that his will had some, even a little, causal efficacy. And so James considered taking control of death, the seemingly most necessary aspect of life, the stupid punch line of this pathetic joke, the part of human existence that seems destined from the start.

According to the *DSM-5*, the *Diagnostic and Statistical Manual of Mental Disorders*, suicidal ideations are a sure sign of a mental disorder. A contemporary of James's, Friedrich Nietzsche, would have disagreed. The thoughts of suicide—thinking carefully about its possibility and meaning—are, for some people, a way of escaping the disorder of existence and putting one's mind back in order. In 1886, in *Beyond Good and Evil*, Nietzsche attests that "the thought of suicide is a great consolation: by means of it one gets successfully through many a bad night."[24] The consolation of this thought can be expressed in at least two ways.

In the words of Martin Buber, suicide can appear as a "trapdoor" or escape hatch. When life is intolerable, the trapdoor can provide some peace of mind: "If things turn utterly hopeless and truly unbearable," I might say, "I don't have to bear them at all. The exit slide is right there. I can always jump."[25] One can marshal on through mass confusion, drudgery, and repression with the lifesaving thought that a dramatic alternative is always available: the uncanny peace of nonexistence.

The contemplation of suicide, however, may be comforting for another, more or less conventional reason. When life is out of control, when it is either too chaotic or too repressive, suicide beckons as the deeply comforting thought that one can, in the end, take the reins by taking one's life. Suicidal role-playing (as we will see, James liked to ingest all sorts of fatal chemicals), failed attempts, and sustained ideations may provide some reassurance that one still has the ability to act on his or her own behalf, to perform an act that is freely chosen precisely because it is radically unthinkable. When James wrote to his father, he was contemplating this Pyrrhic model of suicide: he would win the chance to be free only in hazarding the greatest risk. To be clear, this change was not "necessary" in any fated or absolutely determined fashion. It was, instead, "necessary" only to the extent that James needed, rather desperately, to effect it on his own behalf. He needed to make a decision that mattered. It was necessary—only for him.

Whether suicide was a trapdoor or a Pyrrhic victory, for James it stood as a possible response to circumstances that were beyond his control and not of his choosing. Illness, anxiety, loneliness, and uncertainty culminated in an overwhelming feeling of hopelessness for life and its prospects. His reading of Huxley, in tandem with Darwin and Herbert Spencer, didn't help. They only reinforced his sense that the "emancipated condition" that his mystical father had once achieved was simply beyond him, that human life could not transcend its fated condition.

As James struggled with the idea of determinism, he slowly realized that, in his words, "the stronghold of the deterministic sentiment is the antipathy to the idea of chance." The belief that the universe afforded alternative possibilities—or meaningful chances—disrupted the determinist's strict commitment to the principle of causation. And disruption is the one thing that the determinist cannot abide. According to this view, James writes, "chance is something the notion of which no sane mind can for an instant tolerate in the world."[26] What young James could not tolerate, however, was the pessimism and fatalism entailed by a world devoid of chances.

Determinism's refusal to acknowledge possibility defaces the meaning of free will, James explained, but also vitiates all moral judgments. Remember that every event, for the determinist, even an obviously evil or heinous one, could not have been otherwise. Take the most gruesome murder or hate crime—did the perpetrator mean to do it? Did he or she have a genuine choice in matter? Could he or she have avoided becoming a criminal? Not according to the determinist. In this case, remorse, regret, and moral culpability make very little, if any, sense. There is no use wringing your hands over what might have been or ought to be. The word "ought" presupposes that one has a choice between different possible alternatives. And this is an assumption the determinist will never accept. When it comes to the universe, "it is what it is," nothing more and nothing less. And an individual is powerless to change it. One literally doesn't stand a chance. If this philosophical position makes you deeply uncomfortable, you're not alone. James abhorred it, but in the early 1870s, he was transfixed, paralyzed really, by the deterministic worldview. It was well fit to his study of the empirical sciences and causation in the natural world, but, more immediately, it explained his personal and mental state too perfectly not to be true.

James couldn't shake the sense of his total impotence, but he did manage, for the most part, to hide his depression from his friends and family. When James described the "sick soul" in the *Varieties of Religious Experience* decades later, he still tried to mask the fact that he himself was one of them, disguising it as the report of a mysterious "French correspondent." As James's son, Henry, later revealed, it was really the account of his father's own dire case. James writes that "while in this state of philosophical pessimism and general depression of spirits about my prospects, I went one evening into a dressing room at twilight, to procure some article that was there; when suddenly there fell upon me without warning, just as if it came out of darkness, a horrible fear of my own existence."[27] At the same time, there arose before James a specter of an epileptic patient he had encountered in an asylum. Black-haired, greenish-skinned, knees drawn up to his chest, he sat on a bench "like a sculptured Egyptian cat or Peruvian mummy, moving nothing but his black eyes."[28]

Epilepsy is a chronic disorder. Its effects may temporarily fade, but it is always there. Waiting. Its causes are mysterious, but its symptoms are not—repeated violent convulsions that wrack a body and control entirely the existence of a victim. An epileptic patient is the idea of determinism in human form. James gave one look at the hunched figure, and immediately concluded, "That shape am I."[29] "Nothing that I possess," he continued, "can defend me against that fate, if the hour for it should strike me as it struck him." This realization is never simply temporary, but rather reverberates through the life of the sick soul. James recounted, "I awoke morning after morning with a horrible dread in the pit of my stomach . . . it gradually faded but for months I was unable to go into the dark alone."[30]

Nearly a century before French existentialism overtook Europe, William James was articulating existential anxiety in its most acute forms. The nausea that James experienced would not have been as debilitating had it not stood in such marked contrast to the oblivious optimism that James confronted in his Cambridge surroundings. "I remember wondering how other people," he writes, "could live, how I myself had ever lived, so unconscious of that pit of insecurity beneath the surface of life."[31]

In *Nausea*, Jean-Paul Sartre, who read James extensively in the twentieth century, put a point on this remark: "I am alone in the midst of these happy, reasonable voices. All these creatures spend their time explaining, realizing happily that they agree with each other. In Heaven's name, why is it so important to think the same things all together?"[32] The normalcy of everyday life only heightens the sick soul's alienation, the felt belief that existence on the whole is botched. In James's words, to the sick soul or this "morbid-minded way, as we might call it, healthy-mindedness pure and simple seems unspeakably blind and shallow."[33]

We should be clear—James didn't write about the sick soul in order to give rise to it in his reader. His intention was never to effect existential anxiety or morbid depression. He knew that many healthy-minded people never experience the quietism and despair that he had faced. Good for them. They were the truly lucky ones, the "once-born" who came into the world as babes ready to embrace it.[34] James, however, wanted to acknowledge and describe a much wider range of individuals, with different philosophical outlooks and, often, with different psychological proclivities. In the midst of articulating different attitudes and moral temperaments, James asks to "[p]lease observe, however, that I am not yet pretending finally to *judge* any of these attitudes. I am only describing their variety."[35] For the already healthy-minded, James's account of the sick soul attempts to give them an alternative picture of the selfsame world in which they live. For the fellow sick-souled, it is testament to the fact that they don't suffer in complete isolation. They do, in the words of Arthur Schopenhauer, have a companion in misery: James.

2

Freedom and Life

There is nothing to make one indignant in the
mere fact that life is hard, that men should toil
and suffer pain. The planetary conditions once
for all are such, and we can stand it.

—William James, "The Moral
Equivalent of War," 1906

JAMES RECKONED, AS FEW American thinkers in the
late nineteenth century had, with the prospect of persistent existential disillusionment. His was supposed
to be an age of optimism (not unlike our own) that
was on the verge of reaching the height of enlighten-
ment and happiness. James, however, knew many
intelligent people who thought optimism—and en-
lightenment for that matter—was a sham, and they
experienced a corresponding melancholy that could
only be termed "anhedonia," or the inability to feel
pleasure. In his later descriptions of enduring depression, James would harken back to the low points,
unmoored at sea, on his 1867 trip to the Amazon,

writing, "Prolonged seasickness will in most persons produce a temporary condition of anhedonia. Every good, terrestrial or celestial, is imagined only to be turned from with disgust."[1]

Let's stick to the facts: reality is shot through with despair. Just look around. If one looks carefully, suffering is not the exception but the rule. And the sick-souled tend to look very carefully. They realize what some of the more healthy-minded among us would like to overlook, namely that life, human and otherwise, really does seem to be fated, and not in some Panglossian best-of-all-possible-worlds sort of way. James explains that this impending doom is written into our prehistory: "[T]here is no tooth in any one of those museum-skulls that did not daily through long years of the foretime hold fast to the body struggling in despair of some fated living victim."[2] This is the moral and acutely personal implication of Darwin's survival of the fittest: the weak shall perish, and eventually, given enough time, every being becomes weak. If we look around our immediate surroundings, James suggested, this idea will come home to us in stark relief:

Here on our very hearths and in our gardens the infernal cat plays with the panting mouse, or holds the hot bird fluttering in her jaws. Crocodiles and rattlesnakes and pythons are at this moment vessels of life as real as we are; their loathsome existence fills every minute of every day that drags its length along; and whenever they or other wild beasts clutch their living prey, the deadly horror which an agitated melancholiac feels is the literally right reaction on the situation.[3]

James chose his words carefully: "deadly horror." Yes, it can drive one to leap from a great height or hang oneself from the rafters. It is, however, possible for a melancholiac to live on, but, according to James, it requires a radical transformation when one hits rock bottom. To endure the horror of existence, the sick soul must be "twice born," or reborn in order to love, or at least bear, the act of living.

I've often wondered—in a non-academic way—how this act of psychological resurrection might take place, how it might arise in a person like me. Is it simply a matter of reaching a point in the pit of despair where the only way to go is up? Does the sick soul have to "bottom out," so to speak? There must be something to this, but—I will try to be honest—I don't have a clue about the *exact* nature of the sick soul's rebirth. I can't give a step-by-step account. That being said, I suspect it isn't an experience that can be exhaustively described. Maybe it is something like a second wind; perhaps James was onto this when he supposedly wrote that "most people never run far enough on their first wind to find out they've got a second."[4] But maybe it is more radical than this.

The American naturalist John Muir, a contemporary of James, once told a story of hiking in the Rockies that has helped me picture, if not understand, the twice-born nature of the sick soul, one that reaches a truly impossible impasse the traverse of which suddenly becomes possible. "After gaining a point about half-way to the top," Muir recalled, "I was suddenly brought to a dead stop, with arms outspread, clinging close to the face of the rock, unable to move hand or foot either up or down." This was the crux, according to Muir:

> My doom appeared fixed. I *must* fall. There would be a moment of bewilderment, and then a lifeless rumble down the one general precipice to the glacier below. When this final danger flashed upon me, I became nerve-shaken for the first time since setting foot in the mountain, and my mind seemed to fill with a stifling smoke.[5]

We expect Muir to die in a gruesome accident. He surely expected nothing else—"his doom appeared fixed," and darkness settled in. But then, the climber reported, in the midst of fatalism, he was saved. In Muir's words, "this terrible eclipse lasted only a moment, when . . . I seemed suddenly to become possessed of a new sense. The other self—Instinct, or Guardian Angel—call it what you will—came forward and assumed control." It is not at all clear what or who effected this salvation, but Muir was living proof that he had been rescued from the precipice by a new and overflowing power.

> [M]y trembling muscles became firm again, and every rift and flaw in the rock was seen as through a microscope. My limbs moved with a positiveness and precision with which I seemed to have nothing at all to do. Had I been borne aloft upon wings, my deliverance could not have been more complete.[6]

In our secular society, most people won't believe that Muir was saved by angels, but they might accept that facing death can provide an unexpected and powerful impetus to live. It is precisely in the terrible eclipse of crisis—even suicidal crisis—that one discovers untapped resources. When you survive dying, living doesn't look that bad. Of course, this sort of resurrection isn't guaranteed, but Muir's case suggests that the idea of being reborn in the face of disaster isn't impossible or absurd. There's a chance. Indeed, many people who survive suicidal falls report experiencing immediate regret when their hands release the bridge girder or balcony railing, regret coupled with the almost frantic desire to live. They find the courage to live only when their fate appears wholly sealed.

William James was reborn in the spring of 1870. The exact date is unknown, but an entry from his diary on April 30, 1870, recounts the experience. "I think that yesterday was a crisis in my life. I finished Renouvier's second *Essais* and see no reason why his definition of free will—'the sustaining of a thought because I choose to when I might have other thoughts'—need be the definition of an illusion."[7] The French thinker Charles Renouvier could not be called a "philosopher" by today's standards: he held no academic position; he eschewed formal academic training (the small amount he endured, he claimed, "taught me nothing"); and he wrote prolifically but erratically. He lived, for the most part, a life of reclusion, but there are few thinkers in the nineteenth century who so dramatically affected the course of American pragmatism. He inspired Charles Sanders Peirce, James's lifelong friend, to develop a doctrine of chance known as tychism. Renouvier's role in James's life was even more dramatic—he saved it. Ralph Barton Perry is right in saying that "Renouvier was the single great-est individual influence on James's thought."[8]

Renouvier had studied at the École Polytechnique in Paris while the positivist Augustus Comte had served as an instructor in the Department of Mathe-matics. Comte's full-throated defense of determinism was rivaled only by Huxley's. Positivism held that the point of philosophy—indeed, the point of life—was to achieve objective certainty by sticking exclusively to the physical facts. The observable facts were all a person could, and therefore needed to, know. Positiv-ists left questions of meaning, value, and psychology largely off the table. They were impossible to quan-tify and therefore impossibly vague. Better to rely ex-clusively on the truths that science alone can support. Unfortunately, for thinkers such as Renouvier, this meant neglecting the concepts and ideas that mattered most to human beings, ideas like that of free will.

James's epiphany most likely occurred while read-ing a section of Renouvier's *Essais* entitled "On Lib-erty in Itself." According to the Frenchman, chance—both in the sense of metaphysical randomness but also in the sense of free opportunity—"could not be ex-cluded from the world of concrete affairs." Renouvier writes that an individual's will "could break the logi-cal continuity of a mechanical series and be the ini-tial cause of another series of phenomena."[9] This was the definition of a free act. James was about to try it for the first time. In reading Renouvier, James realized that believing in free will, in an intellectual sense, was not enough, not nearly enough. To truly grasp the lesson of the *Essais*, an action or undertaking was required. The argument for free will might have a proof, but its validity and soundness were only reflected in the activity of life. Upon reading the second *Essais*, James resolved to do something: "My first act of free will," he asserted, "shall be to believe in free will."[10] With these words, James was reborn and his life gradually—in fits and starts—transformed.

In 1871, James took up his scientific studies once again and joined Henry Bowditch in an initiative to found experimental physiology at Harvard Medical School. You'll remember that Bowditch had been James's confidant who listened to him express his "disgust for life" but a year before. But this was a new James. In April of 1872, he received and accepted an informal offer to teach undergraduates at Harvard College, in a course entitled Comparative Anatomy and Physiology. The mundane concerns of adulthood—like bill-paying and supporting a family and selling your soul—played a part in James's decision to accept the instructorship, but they weren't the exclusive, or even most important factors. Teaching would become his vocation, and, with Renouvier's help, he was in the position to respond freely to the calling. He would teach physiology, but in the nineteenth century this discipline opened, almost immediately, into psychology and philosophy. He'd range over all three fields at Harvard for nearly four decades, but feel most at home in philosophy, as he remarked in 1873: "Philosophy I will nevertheless regard as my vocation and never let slip a chance to stroke at it."[11]

James's ability to embrace philosophy was due largely to Renouvier, who had given him a philosophy worth embracing. In one of many notes, James wrote to him, "Thanks to you I possess for the first time an intelligible and reasonable conception of freedom. I accept it almost entirely." His gratitude was not contained to the private sphere, spilling out onto the pages of the *Nation* in a notice of 1873 praising Renouvier's *La critique philosophique*, which stood in marked contrast to the positions of positivism and certain forms of British empiricism. What was remarkable in this little-known text was, in James's words, its hold "to the possibility of absolute beginnings, or free will."[12] In March of that year, James entered his father's house and testified to his own "absolute beginning": "Dear me! What a difference there is between me now and me last spring this time: then so hypochondriacal and now feeling my mind so cleared up and restored to sanity. It is the difference between life and death."[13]

All of this was true, but for a depressive, fair weather is viewed, and even experienced, with intense suspicion. "This cannot possibly be real. This can't be the end of the creeping dis-ease that's dogged me for years. It won't last. Surely this freedom and joy are at best a fluke. At worst, it is a sure sign that things have gotten worse—that I'm completely delusional." A psychological upturn, for a person who rarely enjoys one, can be more unsettling than the condition of perennial sadness. It signals a departure from the norm, and more grievous, the possibility of an unforeseen but imminent relapse. "It is only a matter of time until I feel myself again, namely feel awful." That is the danger of being twice born: there is always the prospect of having to die all over again.

In May of 1873, James took another downturn. Just because you are born again doesn't mean that you don't occasionally feel like dying—again. Renouvier might have been right that free will has some sort of causal efficacy, but James felt himself to be a man "whose trouble seems mainly to be nervous weakness and who craves sedation all the while."[14]

Blessed sleep, the respite insomniacs crave but are never granted—this is what the nervous James desired. He had spent himself teaching his fifty-seven Harvard students during the term and certainly couldn't manage double that number, which his growing fame as an instructor might attract. He just couldn't bear it.

Instead he wrote to his brother Henry, who was currently abroad, asking him to secure a pupil or patron in Italy in the coming months. A winter of recuperation, a break from what James would call the "dreariness of the American condition,"[15] was all he needed to get back on track. As it turns out, this time, he was right: it took a year's vacation in Europe, but James regained his emotional footing again.

James's discovery of Renouvier, and his resulting recovery of free will, appear, at first glance, philosophically suspect. You can believe in free will by simply exercising your free will? Such philosophical bootstrapping seems either self-deceptive or viciously circular. During the mid-1870s, however, James was beginning to consider the possibility that human reason is not, as it had been traditionally regarded, governed strictly by logical dictates. Indeed, certain beliefs can neither be fully deduced nor empirically verified, but life often demands we hold them all the same. For James, believing in free will might not logically be warranted, but it had a profound *practical* worth, and this worth was not separable from the truth-value of the proposition that he came to hold dear: "I am free."

Before being too hard on James for playing fast and loose with belief, consider, just for a moment, the vital truths you hold to be self-evident. I mean the really personal ones that underpin your relationship with others and the world at large. Are they verified or falsified in an exhaustive manner? Are you absolutely sure, and therefore absolutely entitled, to your belief? Are your most cherished ideas about the world objectively certain? James thinks not. We regularly act on behalf of guiding thoughts that function as working hypotheses or the plans for meaningful action. These leading ideas have particular purposes and perform practical work in our lives. This is not to say that belief is "just opinion," although it surely percolates through our everyday opinions, but rather that rationality or the intellect is but one generative force in the creation and maintenance of our ideas. In his essay "The Sentiment of Rationality," which James developed in the late 1870s, he wrote, "Pretend what we may, the whole man within us is at work when we form our philosophical opinions. Intellect, will, taste, and passion cooperate just as they do in practical affairs."[16] Minds are not computers set atop bodies. They are not bloodless calculators that govern our emotions and preferences. As Friedrich Nietzsche wrote in the preface to his *Gay Science*, "We are no thinking frogs, no objectifying and registering devices with refrigerated guts."[17]

As James finally entered adulthood in his midthirties, he arrived at a conclusion, both personal and intellectual: the workings of the human mind are always shot through with attitude, temperament, and volition—the aspects of the human self that had been regarded as fundamentally distinct from our rational powers. He returned to Bowditch's anatomy laboratory at Harvard in 1875 and began to grasp the extent to which the human mind is "embodied," inseparable from bodily lived experience—passionate and affective. When we "change our mind," it is never simply a matter of recognizing the light of reason, but rather altering our entire being. In James's words, "the whole man within us" changes. Similarly, when we "make up our mind" about beliefs and core values, what we really make is a decision about how we will live and what we will become. James made such a choice aided by Renouvier. And in 1876, he did again, this time with the help of a woman by the name of Alice Howe Gibbens.

Falling in love and believing in free will are not all that different. Both are radical, life-altering, working hypotheses, verified or disproved in experience. Both involve the type of belief that one must assent to in an initial act of (basically blind) faith. As a friend once said to me, falling in love, at first, entails no small amount of self-deception, a willingness to act as if you have "all the facts" about your beloved, when in fact you don't.

James didn't know all the facts about Alice Gibbens, but the rumors he heard prior to their meeting in the spring of 1876 were promising. Henry James Sr. had met Alice for the first time at the Radical Club of Boston early that year and, upon returning to the family house at 20 Quincy Street, announced to the James clan that he had met William's future bride. His son really had to meet this remarkable woman. Alice Gibbens was, in the words of her friend the poet John Greenleaf Whittier, a very "American girl," who was "unspoiled by years of sojourn in Europe."[18] Gibbens was a product of the New World: unconventional, even radical, she reflected the social conscience and spiritual curiosity of an increasing number of Boston Brahmins in the decades that followed the Civil War. Like James, Alice was obsessed with freedom, but it meant something quite different for this quiet, rather somber young woman. Whereas the thirty-year-old James understood liberty in terms of a Promethean independence and the "possibility of absolute beginnings," Alice's concerns were more modest but probably much more practical. She was predominantly focused on the chances for freedom in American society, one that was still premised on the subjugation and neglect of workers, racial minorities, women, and children. Socially minded and politically active, Alice struck Henry James Sr. as what nineteenth-century writers might have called an "adjacent soul" to his eldest son, as a beautiful counterpoint to the radical individualism that seized William James's attention after his Renouvier experience.

James was driven by his father's approval of Alice as a suitable match, approval that took the form of a promise of long-standing financial support should James decide to marry her. This, however, is only to suggest the relationship was overdetermined. In the early months of 1876, James was introduced to Alice at the Radical Club by their mutual friend and mentor, the Scottish Aristotelian Thomas Davidson, a philosopher who made his name teaching rather than writing or professing. From the outset, James was totally smitten with Alice, professing his love to her less than a year later in September of 1876:

My dear Miss Gibbens

It seems almost a crime to startle your unconsciousness in the manner in which I am about to do; but seven weeks of insomnia outweigh many scruples, and reflecting on the matter as conscientiously as I can, it seems as if this premature declaration were fraught with less evil than any of the other courses possible to me now. To state abruptly the whole matter: I am in love, *und zwar* [namely] (—forgive me—) with Yourself.[19]

Today this declaration of love is often regarded as the opening gambit in a permanent romance. Once the initial move has been made, it is up to the beloved to reciprocate or not; the lover is simply to await the response. James's willfulness, however, could not abide this sort of passivity. He explained to Alice, "My duty in my own mind is clear. It is to win your hand, if I can."[20] Now, what he needed from her was a formal permission to try: "What I beg of you now," James wrote, "is that you should let me know categorically whether any absolute irrevocable obstacle already exists to that consummation." This isn't exactly the sexiest way to fall in love—in fact, it is not like "falling" at all—but it was the only way James knew how to commit. He had to will it, work at it, win it.

Alice was game—almost too eager, in fact. In the months after writing this note, James, in typical form, made things hard on himself, and now on Alice. For a man constantly worried about the efficacy of free will, self-sabotage became a form of testing his volition. It was as if a real struggle were required in order to prove (more to himself than anyone else) that the union was freely chosen. James had spent much of his life believing that he was dispositionally unfit for marriage. He was too weak, too sickly, too psychologically unstable, to be a good partner to anyone. How could he ask anyone else to permanently bear his company when *he* could hardly stand himself? On the brink of marriage, these self-doubts multiplied and intensified. After James had won her hand, he attempted to convince Alice that his wasn't worth holding, writing to her that he could produce "undreamed of arguments *against* accepting any offer I may make."[21] Alice, despite his warnings, still accepted his offer, and James, after several false starts, announced in May 1878 that he was engaged.

Some sick souls never get to this point. We remain disengaged by choice, or chance, or constitutional necessity. Maybe we live in mortal fear of rejection. Maybe we are so fixated on our own obsessions and drawbacks that we fail to notice our neighbors, friends, and potential loved ones. Maybe we simply can't believe that someone else would be willing to fall in love with us. Maybe we refuse to join a club that would ever grant us admittance. Maybe we flirt, as James did, with all of these thoughts. To overcome them, for some of us, remains that task of a lifetime.

On the twenty-year anniversary of meeting Alice, James delivered what many people regard as his most famous lecture: "The Will to Believe." This address, given to the Divinity School at Yale in June of 1896, is usually understood as a contribution to the philosophy of religion, an argument for voluntarily adopted faith. When empirical evidence is insufficient to prove the reality of the Divine, James argued that one could still will belief, and that this move does not violate the strictures of reason. The belief itself, according to James, can change a believer's world such that the belief is validated over time. When one believes in God, even in the absence of exhaustive proof (because after all, how many of us can really attest to having exhaustive proof?), his or her reality lends itself more readily to religious experience.

What is often overlooked in commentaries on "The Will to Believe" is the way that this lynchpin of classical American philosophy applies to the maintenance of meaningful human relations, relations that can be lost on the sick souls of the world. James was speaking directly to such a relationship, to his relationship with his twenty-year love, Alice. James agrees with Pascal that in the case of certain questions, "the heart has reasons that reason cannot know," but he believes that such questions are never restricted to theology. Instead these questions repeatedly emerge in practical affairs—moral and interpersonal—of nonbelievers. In concluding "The Will to Believe," James argues that while questions of religion and morality might not resonate with everyone, one very basic question will be important for the vast majority of people: "Do you like me or not?" This was the question that James so desperately needed Alice to answer. Indeed, it is a question that underpins large swaths of human sociality. And it is a question that cannot be answered in any a priori or exhaustive way. But time is of the essence. One has to act before one really knows the answer. Goethe, one of James's literary heroes, puts it best: "What you can do, or dream you can do, begin it. Boldness has genius, power and magic in it."[22] Looking back on his initial meeting with Alice, James urges us to "begin it," to exercise our will in the face of uncertainty, writing,

> Whether you [like me] or not depends, in countless instances, on whether I meet you half-way, am *I willing to assume* that you must like me and show trust and expectation. The previous faith on my part in

your liking's existence is in such cases what makes your liking come. But if I stand aloof, and refuse to budge an inch until I have objective evidence, until you shall have done something apt, as the absolutists say, *ad extorquendum assensum meum*, ten to one your liking never comes.[23]

When it comes to love, there is nothing *ad extorquendum assensum meum*, nothing to "force my assent." I have to give my assent before sufficient logical justification is supplied, and when I do, the evidence, it is hoped, begins to trickle in. If there was any doubt that he was talking explicitly about matters of romance, James exclaimed, "How many women's hearts have been vanquished by the mere sanguine insistence of one man that they must love him!" Now this, I admit, is pretty gross—the idea that women acquiesce in the face of a bold (read masculine) imperative. This is not, even James knows, how love works. The point is subtler. Paring back the apparent chauvinism, he explains in more measured terms:

> The desire for a certain kind of truth here brings about that special truth's existence; and so it is in innumerable cases of other sorts. Who gains promotions, boons, appointments, but the man in whose life they are seen to play the part of live hypotheses, who discounts them, sacrifices other things for their

> sake before they have come, and takes risks for them
> in advance? His faith acts on the powers above him
> as a claim, and creates its own verification.[24]

This isn't just a matter of wishful thinking or outright delusion. All sick souls who have done battle with themselves for any extended period of time have received the vapid advice to "buck up," to "just smile," to "look on the bright side." James is not giving this kind of pointer, but rather explaining the underlying architecture of belief, which might make this advice meaningful. He is explaining how a certain sort of truth—like the truth about love—comes to be. It doesn't just emerge fully formed in the head of a lover or beloved. Instead, it grows—or doesn't—between two people in their actively meeting halfway. And this communion requires a bit of faith, or at minimum an act of optimism. James knows that "looking on the bright side" is often not objectively warranted: life is harsh and cruel in all of the ways that the sick soul suspects. It is, however, practically warranted, deeply useful as what he called a "live hypothesis." Acting *as if* the world is a welcoming and tender place occasionally has the effect of making it more so.

I was, and still am, socially awkward. Today, my full-time job is to "profess" philosophy to large groups, but for most of my life the one thing that made me more uncomfortable than public speaking was, well, large groups. As a kid I was too big to be fast and not big enough to be strong. I was uncoordinated and stuttered badly. I was scared of going to other kids' birthday parties and terrified of recess—but at least when you got beat up or teased at a birthday party you could eat cake. I wasn't exactly popular. Soon I wasn't invited to most of the birthday parties. When I was seven, my mother noticed that I still had a number of very good imaginary friends, and was more comfortable playing with them in my head than with any real ones on the playground. I was, as a small saving grace, a pretty imaginative youngster. My mom, a counseling psychologist who had studied James and cognitive behavioral therapy, took me aside two years later: "John, I know you don't like recess," she said. "I know you don't really get along with a bunch of the kids. But could you pretend like you do? Just for a month? Just pretend and see what happens." So I put on a good show: I smiled, said hello, learned to laugh at myself, played the games I didn't actually suck at, and pretended my way into a very few lasting friendships. Perhaps this was my first of many experiments in what self-help gurus sometimes call "the power of positive thinking." "Be the change you want to see in the world," I can hear the healthy-minded mentor say—but as a sick soul, I can hardly read these words without retching. In hindsight, I think my mother was encouraging something a little different, something like "fake it till you make it": will yourself to act in a certain manner, and your volition may alter, in positive ways, the state of affairs.

Of course, sometimes you fake it but really don't make it. The same mother who saved me from a *Lord of the Flies* version of childhood also advised me into my first marriage. On the morning of the wedding, she and I went for a car ride in rural central Pennsylvania, a last pep talk before the main event. I needed it. I told her that I really wasn't at all sure about what I was about to get into. She said it was just nerves. She said that I just needed to buckle down and invest in the relationship. She said, "Marriage is hard—and getting into it, by way of a wedding, isn't easy either." Just do it. Just commit to the plan and make it happen. "It will happen," Mom said as we got back to town and changed into fancy clothes. "Trust yourself."

Self-trust has its limits. Sometimes when you will yourself to believe, you are, in fact, making a very big mistake. I filed for divorce on my thirtieth birthday. I don't blame my mother. Her advice reflected what I now see is an essential truth about relationships: that volition is a necessary condition in their establishment

and maintenance. I know this because I was married—
for a second time—for a decade. Enduring love doesn't
just happen, and it, for most people, isn't girded by
convention or tradition alone. Volition, however, is
a necessary, but not sufficient, condition of love. James
and my mother were not suggesting that you enter a
romance with your eyes shut tightly. Instead they were
merely observing that one rarely has all the facts be-
forehand and, in many instances, one must act and
commit well before the verdict is in. "Just do it." But
realize that things might not go well. This isn't the
same thing as fixating on your potential failure—
which is what I am wont to do—which will invari-
ably stifle your chances altogether. It is only to be realistic about the nature of living hypotheses; they are
still contingent on the vagaries and frailty of human
life. That is inescapable but not lamentable.

Over the years, I have come to believe that there is
something deeply, if not divinely, right about situations that require James's will to believe. Being in
love is not like falling from a great height, or, as the
theologian Thomas Merton writes, like tripping into
a deep pool.[25] It is not passively experienced. It involves a free act, with one eye open, that can, and
usually does, transform a life for better or for ill, for
richer or for poorer. Love's conditions are partially up
to you. This means that you have the power to effect

a romance, but are also fated to be effected by it. Remember: *partially* up to you. If love were fail-safe or prearranged, it wouldn't mean nearly so much when it survives.

In 1878, with Alice's encouragement, James discovered that freedom can, to echo Robert Frost, lie in the power of being bold.[26] Determinism didn't hold, at least when it came to the felt experience of taking meaningful and novel action. James took a chance at being in love, and, this time, with a bit of luck and work, it took solid root. Once the human will is exercised with success or reinforcement, it is primed for future opportunities. As he finalized his marital plans with Alice, James also finagled his way into an elusive permanent appointment at Harvard, in philosophy no less, a discipline that attracted pitifully few in the scientifically minded circles of modern academia. In the spring of 1878, he signed a contract with Henry Holt for a textbook that was supposed to revolutionize the field of modern psychology—it was to be grounded in empirical sciences but avoid reductionism and, ultimately, determinism. The publisher wanted the manuscript in a single year. James thought this was slightly too ambitious, but he could deliver it in two if he started immediately. This was meant to be a reasonable compromise, but it turned out to be a wildly hopeful promise. He misgauged the time line—by about a decade—but he did start immediately on the undertaking.

When the wedding of James and Alice concluded in June of 1878, the newlyweds retreated to the Keene valley in the Adirondacks for their honeymoon, and James began to work on the *Principles of Psychology* as if anything were possible. More accurately, as James's friend Francis Child remarked to James Russell Lowell, "they [meaning Alice and James] are both writing it."[27] Alice would be his partner in most things from that point forward. In the fall of that year, after a summer of honeymooning and studying, the *Psychology* was begun and Alice was pregnant. James had discovered, after more than thirty tenuous years, that chance often begets chance.

3

Psychology and the Healthy Mind

My thinking is first and last and always for
the sake of my doing.
—William James, *The Principles of
Psychology*, 1890

AT THIS POINT IN OUR STORY, one might reasonably
expect for things to go well. By 1879, James had temporarily vanquished the threats of determinism, and
it looked, at least from the outside, like he'd realized
a degree of personal freedom and control in a life that
occasionally teetered on the abyss. He had, for the
time being, stepped back from the edge—landing a
perfect job, marrying the perfect wife, and finally, after
many unsuccessful years, managing to satisfy his sub-
tly exacting father. All he had to do was settle into
his new life and secure his happiness. Securing one's
happiness, however, is no easy matter. James had entered the Harvard rat race and now he had to run. His
father—and now his colleagues—expected him to go

places, to be truly great. Anything less would be a complete failure.

The *Principles*, the project that consumed his forties, was beyond ambitious. Yes, James wanted the challenge, but he also *thought* it had to be momentous. At this point in his life, he had to do something of consequence. The task was twofold—to make the budding field of psychology accountable to the most rigorous methods of the natural sciences and to simultaneously explain how this empirical study of the human mind avoided scientific reductionism. If this weren't enough, James wrote the *Principles of Psychology* to answer—as a modern scientist would—one of the oldest questions of philosophy: How does life give rise to human consciousness? As the pre-Socratic Parmenides might have said, "What is the relationship between Being and Thinking?" The task was beyond ambitious. Crazy, really. The fact that there were no modern labs to do the experiments that *might* generate the findings that *might* underpin James's project was beside the point. He would just have to do the experiments himself. He *had* to succeed, or die trying. Those were the only options.

James was intent on being somebody, which often makes being happy rather difficult. Beginning in the 1880s, he began to shuttle his family between financial largess and paucity, entering a relationship with money and fame that bordered on the dysfunctional. There was always a lot of both, but never enough of either. Of course, this situation is common enough today, but it being common really doesn't make it any less soul-sucking. Remember that "goddess Success," whom James had tried to avoid for so long? She was in complete control now.

I shouldn't overstate the discontent that James felt as he embarked on the *Principles of Psychology*. There are people—some, many, most, or all—who thrive on a bit of dis-ease, the feeling of striving for something, the sense, in James's words, that experience remains "ever not quite." This is just part of our biology: if you think about a cell, the only time it reaches perfect stasis or equilibrium—"perfect balance" as the gurus might say—is when it is dead. Life happens on the move, and James, more than most, was determined to stay alive.

As he began to develop the opening chapters of *The Principles*, James remarked to Alice, "I have often thought the best way to define a man's character would be to seek out the particular mental or moral attitude in which, when it came upon him, he felt himself most deeply and intensely alive. At such moments there is a voice inside that speaks and says, '*This* is the real me.'"[1] Here's the rub: adult life makes tracking down the "real me" extremely tricky. We may grow older linearly, year by year, but the sheer number of obligations and expectations that fill our days increases exponentially. Strangely, this doesn't mean that we necessarily feel, in James's words, "deeply and intensely alive." Instead, the business of living becomes no more than numbing busyness; we are pulled, once again, in many directions without dedicating ourselves to any one activity. And we negotiate the morass of everyday life precisely by "shutting down" and "tuning out," by going on psychological autopilot. This makes routinized action sound wholly negative. It's not. It is a survival mechanism, a heuristic or set of shortcuts, which allows us to quickly act without thinking. There is, however, a problem with this shortcut. It often allows one to forget—or to forget even how—to ask which "particular mental attitude" harbors the "real me." James discovered this in his forties as he crafted the *Principles*. It was a personal insight regarding the dangers of midlife, coupled with a detailed scholarly investigation of one of the root causes of these dangers: the irrepressible but subterranean force of habit.

"Habit" has always been the watchword in Western self-help culture. Aristotle, in the fourth century BCE, anticipated our obsession with the word: "We are what we repeatedly do. Excellence is not an act. It is a habit."[2] Today we try, often unsuccessfully, to break bad habits—smoking, texting, compulsive shopping, procrastination, sleeping late, gambling, lying, and cheating on our partner. We strive to form good ones—working out, paying attention, working hard, waking early, saving money, telling the truth, playing fair, and being faithful. The ubiquitous nature of habit was clear to James, who wrote,

> When we look at living creatures from an outward point of view, one of the first things that strikes us is that they are bundles of habits. In wild animals, the usual round of daily behavior seems a necessity implanted at birth; in animals domesticated, and especially in man, it seems, to a great extent, to be the result of education. The habits to which there is an innate tendency are called instincts; some of those due to education would by most persons be called acts of reason. It thus appears that habit covers a very large part of life, and that one engaged in studying the objective manifestations of mind is bound at the very outset to define clearly just what its limits are.[3]

By the time James wrote the *Principles of Psychology* in the mid-1880s, everyone knew that habit was important in the living of a good life. What remained a mystery was the exact process by which habits took hold in what James called the "objective manifestations of mind." That was what James set out to explain in the fourth chapter of the *Principles*, in an argument so compelling that the chapter was republished and widely circulated as a stand-alone book. He believed that by laying habit bare and revealing its inner workings, he could help his reader harness, and to some extent control, its power. It was, for James, as most of his studies were, a means of getting a grip on himself. James had outgrown Bowditch's physiology labs, so in the lead-up to the publishing of the *Principles* in 1890 he founded his own, focusing his small staff on the physical basis of the human mind. Obviously, they rarely used humans as their experimental subjects. James's specialty at the time was comparative anatomy: he had to content himself with frogs, dogs, cats, and the occasional monkey.

Minds of all kinds, James discovered, are pliable things, not exactly fragile, but not exactly rigid either. Conscious life, in all its forms, James maintained, is defined by thoroughgoing plasticity, which he defined as "a structure weak enough to yield to an influence, but strong enough not to yield all at once." It is meant, or has evolved, to bend but not to break. "Each relatively stable phase of equilibrium in such a structure," James continues, "is marked by what we may call a new set of habits."[4] The equilibrium of habit is not a perfect and enduring stillness, but a temporary stable phase, in which an organism's conscious life and its surroundings achieve a certain "fit" for the time being. I sometimes tease my students that they always sit in the same seats—even without me assigning them. Week after week, a student finds his or her own desk. By the fifth meeting, I don't have to use my seating chart. Everyone has come to know his or her place. This habit, like all habits, has a physical signature: it feels good deep down in our flesh and bones. And it works well enough, until a new student attends and, heaven forbid, *takes* someone else's seat. The habit is disrupted. Then all hell breaks loose. This is pretty funny—to see young adults argue over who sits where—but I don't laugh too loudly. If my students take a few classes with me, they will come to know that I am a deeply habitual creature. I have a cup of coffee in the morning, every morning. Maybe I also tell them that at five o'clock, every evening, without fail, I have a beer. This is a deeply functional habit. It is the point of the day when I have pretty much "had it." Even if it has been a beautiful, relatively easy day, I've had it. The sunshine is sometimes just too brutal. My beer takes the edge off: so that life doesn't cut so harshly, so that I'm not so sharp with others. Sure, I could say that I just like to have a beer in the evening, but this wouldn't be true and it wouldn't capture the nature of my habit. I've come to a relatively stable phase of equilibrium when it comes to beer and my everyday life. Beer and my life just fit.

When we think about a deeply engrained habit—like my beer drinking—it is easy to focus on the stability of the situation. But what we tend to overlook in this emphasis is the way that the establishment of habits relies on an underlying, and remarkable, flexibility. In his 1887 "The Law of Habit," James writes that "[o]rganic matter, especially nervous tissue, seems endowed with a very extraordinary degree of plasticity ... so that we may without hesitation lay down as our first proposition the following, that *the phenomena of habit in living beings are due to plasticity of the organic materials of which their bodies are composed*."[5] This proposition comes very close to anticipating Hebb's rule, articulated by cognitive scientist Donald Hebb in 1949, that neurons that "fire together, wire together."[6] In other words, the activation of certain neural pathways alters the physical and chemical makeup of an organism such that similar activations are more likely in the future. This is known as "priming" and is an important factor in the early stages of establishing habits, good or otherwise.

If you don't feel like your mind is as supple as it used to be, you're probably right. James observed that the cognitive architecture of young bodies is more pliable, and therefore more open to habit formation, than old ones. "Could the young but realize how soon they will become mere walking bundles of habits," James lamented, "they would give more heed to their conduct while in the plastic state. We are spinning our own fates, good or evil, and never to be undone."[7] Nervous systems, like our own, are not hardwired from the start (what fun would that be?) but rather artifacts of our evolutionary and experiential histories. And they remain open to new impressions, in varying degrees, right up to the end, when everything goes black for an organism. That being said, we are most susceptible to influence, most malleable, in early adolescence, namely when we have the *least* amount of control over our surroundings and our lives. We might be spinning our own fate, as James said, but at the outset we are pretty clueless weavers.

For a man intent on exercising his freedom, this investigation of habit could have been very disturbing. Indeed, at times, it seems to have bothered James deeply. It suggested that the great ballast of human cognition—what allows us to stay upright in the face of a turbulent and complex world—is a growing bundle of routines and scripts that we acquire as second nature. Habit is essentially conservative. It keeps things the same, in place, for as long as possible. In

James's words, "Habit is thus the enormous fly-wheel of society, its most precious conservative agent." James concluded that

> [habit] alone is what keeps us all within the bounds of ordinance, and saves the children of fortune from the envious uprisings of the poor. It alone prevents the hardest and most repulsive walks of life from being deserted by those brought up to tread therein. It keeps the fisherman and the deck-hand at sea through the winter; it holds the miner in his darkness, and nails the countryman to his log cabin and his lonely farm through all the months of snow; it protects us from invasion by the natives of the desert and the frozen zone. It dooms us all to fight out the battle of life upon the lines of our nurture or our early choice, and to make the best of a pursuit that disagrees, because there is no other for which we are fitted, and it is too late to begin again.[8]

There was a certain resoluteness to this assessment. It's sad, but not necessarily pessimistic (as many of the observations of the young James had been). Only jarringly realistic. An organism can satisfy itself—is *built* to satisfy itself—in some pretty despicable conditions. Many animals, humans perhaps most especially, often prefer self-defeating habits to explicit danger, even if that danger might be a means to a more healthy, vibrant life. Many friendships, many relationships, survive by no other virtue than this.

In the early 1880s, James began to shift his analysis of the human condition. It was an adjustment in perspective rather than any radical reevaluation of the facts of existence. His writing, despite being tinged with the memories and experiences of the sick soul, began to be increasingly well adjusted. His experiments on, and conclusions regarding, habit could have sent him into another psychological tailspin. Indeed, they often threatened to. But, in this case, James rebounded, insisting that habit could be rejected, or more modestly, that its effects could be monitored and therefore kept from overrunning life. This too seems to be a way of maintaining freedom. If life is largely governed by habit, by the semiconscious workings of instinct and routine, then the least we can do as free agents is understand how we are constrained. Many a determinist had proposed precisely this position, and in the early stages of the *Principles of Psychology*, James seems to be veering toward the conclusion the seventeenth-century idealist Baruch Spinoza put forward, that the highest activity of human life is learning for the sake of understanding the world and ourselves, because, in short, to understand is to be free. Perhaps by understanding the strictures on freedom, one could eke out a semblance of independence.

This Stoic response, however, would not satisfy the mature James. In the end, the point of life was to recognize the power of habit, but then to guide it and overcome it. James concludes his analysis of habit by underscoring its possible transcendence, writing in the *Principles*, "Genius, in truth, means little more than the faculty of perceiving in an *unhabitual* way."[9] Following his friend and mentor Ralph Waldo Emerson, James believes that every individual is imbued with this rare and beautifully disruptive faculty. We just have to exercise it. And when we do, and when we are lucky, we embrace habits that enliven and strengthen rather than bore and cripple us. On the heels of the *Principles*, James wrote that individuals who had long adhered to docile, self-defeating habits could, in fact, live otherwise. They could adopt new routines. James writes,

Fifteen years ago the Norwegian women were even more than the women of other lands votaries of the old-fashioned ideal of femininity, "the domestic angel," the "gentle and refining influence" sort of thing. Now these sedentary fireside tabby-cats of Norway have been trained, they say, by the snowshoes into lithe and audacious creatures, for whom no night is too dark or height too giddy, and who are not only saying good-bye to the traditional feminine

pallor and delicacy of constitution, but actually taking the lead in every educational and social reform. I
cannot but think that the tennis and tramping and
skating habits and the bicycle-craze which are so rap-
idly extending among our dear sisters and daughters
in this country are going also to lead to a sounder and
heartier moral tone, which will send its tonic breath
through all our American life.[10]

I'm not sure if the habit of exercise and play—for
those who had been denied the opportunity of both—
leads to "a heartier moral tone." But it sure as hell
can lead to a better life, or at the very least, a different type of life. I know: some people can't ski or play
tennis or ride a bike. I get it. I am not being an able-
ist, but I do agree with James that most people have
options when it comes to the activities that govern
their lives. Even small variations can matter a great
deal. Habits are often the things that we "inherit,"
loosely put, from our parents and our teachers. But
James reminds us that they don't always have to be.
Maybe it can be up to us.

James was a remarkably unconventional creature.
The American philosopher and my teacher Doug Anderson likes to say that he was an "undercover Roman
candle"—a violent explosive concealed beneath the
trappings of an Ivy League life. Anderson is right: few

thinkers have been more sensitive to the feeling of being cramped or constrained by the forces of habit. Even as he fell under the sway of adulthood, James continued to have an almost allergic reaction to the mundane niceties and routines that were expected in his Cambridge neighborhood. According to his son, when the James household hosted a conventional dinner party, his father would often disappear in an Irish Goodbye, abandoning his guests without bidding them farewell, retreating to his study for a bit of free time. In 1885, weighed down by the writing of the *Principles*, James wrote to Shadworth Hodgeson, "I need to lead a purely animal life for at least two months to carry me through the teaching year."[11] James had to feel that he was breaking free—if only for a little while—in order to survive being normal. It was just who he was.

Perhaps this strikes you as a juvenile unwillingness to shoulder the duties of modern life, a petulant refusal to curb one's sense of adventure long enough to be a responsible adult. And perhaps you are totally right: James was not, by any stretch of the imagination, a homemaker or family man. He left managing the house entirely to Alice and generally eschewed the tedious bits of rearing their five children. But I will say this for James: he was quite transparent about who he was, and how much he hated the doldrums of what he took to be stultifying habits. At least he was honest about it. In the letter to Alice regarding the pursuit of the "real me," James explained that his essential identity was an essentially vexed one:

> Now as well as I can describe this . . . real me . . . this characteristic attitude in me always involves an active tension, of holding my own, as it were and trusting outward things to perform their part so as to make it a full harmony, but without any *guaranty* that they will. Make it a guaranty—and the attitude immediately becomes to my consciousness stagnant and stingless.[12]

The world of lockstep habit—in which every position, every seat, every moment is guaranteed and perfectly ordered—was not a world that could accommodate James's "real me." Instead, James wrote, indeed, pled: "take away the guarantee." As soon as this wish was granted and the world was again opened to real chance and real opportunity, James reported, "I feel (provided I am *überhaupt* in vigorous condition) a sort of deep enthusiastic bliss." James was informing his new bride that she had just committed herself to a man who did not endure, but actually relished, risk taking.

It was also, I suspect, a not-so-subtle request. James was asking his partner not to impinge on her husband's sense of "real me." He seems to suggest: "Be not afraid of life," for it is only in risking ourselves that we find out what we can become. Of course, it is far easier to live on the edge, so to speak, if your wife protects you from distraction and triviality. I do, however, think there is something to James's comment that living life in tension can be deeply meaningful. In his words, when confronted with a world of possibility and given the choice about its future, he was struck by "a willingness to do and suffer anything, which translates itself physically by a kind of stinging pain inside my breastbone . . . and which although it is a mere mood or emotion . . . authenticates itself to me as the deepest principle of all."[13] For some, human existence matters most when we set goals and strive for undetermined outcomes. Maybe we will fail. Maybe not. But in either case, it will be *our* failure and *our* triumph—and that ownership matters.

When I was going through my first divorce, I read *The Principles of Psychology* again. I also went through James's letters, just to see what he was thinking about during the time. There were a lot of letters, but it turns out that one has more time to read when one is alone and doesn't get up until noon. I remember sitting in bed and thinking that all of James's heroic talk about overcoming self-effacing habits by a sheer act of will struck me as unrealistic and, in my condition, a bit mean-spirited. I couldn't even *feel* differently much less *act* differently. What I felt was only the intense urge to stay in my goddamn bed—and that was not going to change.

It eventually did change. I remembered that James's comment to Alice about the "real me" had a serious proviso: he said that "the deep enthusiastic bliss" of struggle, the tension that signaled his true self, could only be felt when he was "*überhaupt* in vigorous condition." That is to say, generally in good condition. Even in later life, James was no stranger to debilitating feelings. As he honed his thoughts on the nature of habit, in 1884, James wrote to his life-long tutor, the Scotsman Thomas Davidson, admitting that "teaching duties have really devoured the whole of my time this winter and with hardly any intellectual profit whatever. I have read nothing, and written nothing save one lecture on the freedom of the will. How it is going to end, I don't well see."[14] This is not an isolated complaint. A brief survey of his letters reveals an abiding uneasiness in the life of William James: he was a busy bee, but beneath the industry were persistent feelings of stagnation and impotence.

How is one to get rid—or at least deal—with these feelings? As David Foster Wallace said in 2005, how do you make "it to thirty, or even fifty, without wanting to shoot yourself in the head?"[15] That is the question that plagued me through my first marriage and culminated when the relationship finally came apart. Even after the disaster of the divorce, I was, objectively speaking, still in pretty good shape: I had a job teaching philosophy, a solid income, one or two close friends, and more or less my health. These objective facts of life (the events that could be studied from the outside), however, did absolutely nothing to quell my stay-in-bed-all-day feeling.

Feelings are usually regarded as the most private of mental states, the shadows that occupy the deepest recesses of our minds. My feelings are mine and definitely not yours. James's analysis of his true self turns, in a certain sense, on the interiority of feeling. That which he *feels* most acutely, *feels* under his breastbone, must be the "real me." Our feelings are what make each of us special—especially upbeat, especially sensitive, especially volatile—just special. There is, however, a slight problem with this model of human emotion, articulated by Amy Tan, the author of *The Joy Luck Club*, who writes, "Our uniqueness makes us special, makes perception valuable—but it can also make us lonely. This loneliness is different than being 'alone' . . . the feeling I am talking about stems from the sense that we can never fully share the truth of who we are."[16]

I remember a colleague checking up on me the day before the papers were signed. He came to my apartment, strewn with books and dirty dishes and bottles of all sorts. He stayed for an hour, and then left me with just two words: "Feel better." He uttered them as if from a great distance, as if he were wishing that someone, far away, would finally end world hunger. I think he believed that my feelings, whatever they were, were in some deep, unreachable place—inside me. He couldn't get to them. He could have given me a hug or taken me for a walk. But he didn't. He probably thought that touching or moving my body would do very little to affect my battered feelings, hidden as they were. As it turns out, he was wrong.

In the penultimate chapter of the *Principles*, entitled "The Emotion," James explains that most basic human feelings are not strictly, or even primarily, internal. They aren't just "in our heads" so to speak. An emotion is not a ghost in a machine or some enigmatic force that drives us through our daily affairs. Instead, it is always tightly bound to our actions and bodily states, and not in the way that we typically think. For most of my life, I thought that when I was hopelessly antisocial, or wallowing around my messy house, or failing to get out of bed, it was because I was depressed. Nope. James suggests it is the other way around: I feel sad because I constantly look at my shoes while in public, because my house is dimly lit and cramped, because I fail to stand upright. In his words, "We don't laugh because we're happy, we're happy because we laugh."[17] The action itself is enough to bring about a particular affective state.

James had studied physiology long enough to begin to understand what today we call "biofeedback," the mutual reinforcement of the expression of emotion and its subjective feeling, and he had concluded, for a number of different reasons, that certain bodily activities and responses gave rise to the "coarser emotions": regret, anger, fear, and joy. This is at the core of what became known as the James-Lange theory of emotion. James held that an emotion, devoid of expression and practical consequence, is largely meaningless:

> If we fancy some strong emotion, and then try to abstract from our consciousness of it all the feelings of its bodily symptoms, we find that we have nothing left behind. . . . Can one fancy the state of rage and picture no ebullition in the chest, no flushing of the face, no dilation of the nostrils, no clenching of the

teeth, no impulse to vigorous action . . . ? The present writer, for one, cannot.[18]

Goethe was right—"Boldness has magic." And the magic of human activity is not just in its ability to change our circumstances, to transform the surroundings in which we live. No small part of the magic has to do with the way that activity can radically alter the emotional landscape of our inner lives. According to James, our passions don't hijack our decisions and actions; rather our actions can either give our emotions free rein or keep them in check. The James-Lange theory ran against the grain of conventional thinking, but its founders thought the empirical evidence was decidedly in their favor. In the *Principles*, James explains that "panic is increased by flight," "sobbing makes . . . sorrow more acute," and "in rage . . . we work ourselves up . . . by repeated outbreaks."[19] In many cases, a refusal to express the emotion is the first step in letting the passion pass. At the age of thirty, having contributed my share to a self-destructive relationship, I had to admit that James might have been on to something. Just clenching my teeth is a surefire way to get much, much angrier.

I remember finally reaching the end of the *Principles* and thinking that the preceding thousand pages had led me to this point in "The Emotions": "sit all day in a moping posture," James writes, "sigh, and reply to everything with a dismal voice, and your melancholy lingers . . . smooth your brow, brighten your eye, contract the dorsal rather than the ventral aspect of the frame . . . and your heart must be frigid indeed if not to generally thaw!"[20] After we finalized the divorce, I read, and reread, this passage. It primed me to accept an invitation that I would have rejected a year earlier. I had another colleague. Thank God it wasn't the "feel better" guy. This other colleague invited me to a yoga class. I was not, in any way, shape, or form, a yogi. I was, if anything at that point, a gym rat, and gym rats don't bend or twist easily. I didn't want to go, but I did, remembering James's words that I would "cold-bloodedly" have to go through the motions of being happier in order to actually become so.

Many people, beginning with my first wife, suggested that I give yoga a shot. "It'll really calm you down," she'd say. I just pictured myself in a sarong, sitting in lotus, seething. No thanks. My colleague promised this would be different—we'd move and sweat a bunch. I'd be so busy catching my breath and concentrating on not falling down that I wouldn't have the chance to think about my thoughts or my shitty life. That didn't sound so horrible. No one would be in a sarong. I'd only have to sit still at the end of session, and by then, she promised, I'd be deeply grateful for the break. So I agreed, and met her at the crack of dawn at the neighborhood studio in Boston's North End.

"Smooth the brow, brighten the eye, contract the dorsal rather than the ventral aspect of the body." These are James's words from the *Principles*, but they could basically be the cues for Surya Namaskara A, the basic sun salutation in Ashtanga Yoga. Calm your face, set your intention with your brightened eye, stand straight with your chest out and shoulders squared, now go: Bend at the waist, place your hands on the floor, and step back so that your body is a stiff plank. Lower the plank to the ground. Now look up. Way up. Tighten that dorsal aspect of your body. Now contract your gut muscles like you are laughing, and stick your butt in the air so your body makes an upside-down "V." This is "downward-facing dog." Hang out here for a few breaths and let the fresh blood rush to your head. Relax your face. Relax. Now jump your feet to your hands. And use every single one of those dorsal muscles to stand you up from the waist. Raise your hands and look up like your life depends on it. Repeat the whole cycle. Repeat. Repeat. Repeat.

By the fourth salutation I was drenched in my own juices. This prescribed set of bodily movements had done something to my emotional malaise. Things were definitely looking up. A student is only supposed to do five sun salutations in the primary series of Ashtanga. But I was hooked. I went home that first day and did a hundred—in a little more than three hours. They were horrible looking, I am sure. But standing up straight, repeatedly, was addictive. I couldn't move for a week, but when I did, I called my friend back and asked if she might like to go to a yoga class *with me*. Wasn't Ashtanga a little too rigid? Maybe a vinyasa—a class that links breath to movement—with an insane number of Sun As would do the trick. She agreed. We went every day, twice a day, for two months. Then once a day for a year.

James's friend Wincenty Lutoslawski was a yoga fanatic, and James wrote to him in the twilight of life that "[y]our whole narrative suggests in one whether the Yoga discipline may not be, after all, in all of its phases, a methodical way of waking up deeper levels of will power than are habitually used, and thereby increasing an individual's vital tone and energy."[21] This is, even for the novice yogi, the truth of the matter. Over time, yoga became a Jamesian habit, but it also became a type of emotional and physical spring training for the rest of my life. "Everybody should do at least two things each day that he hates to do, just for practice," James instructs. He knew, secondhand, that yoga could be one of these things.

My colleague Carol taught me yoga and indeed many things. We eventually moved in together and decided to get married. Today we have a beautiful seven-year-old daughter. James, however, would caution against anticipating the future in any lockstep fashion. The future is not determined. Many beautiful stories have unexpected endings. After ten years, Carol and I filed for our own divorce, and are now trying to raise our daughter in the midst of this schism (which I am sure is a book for another time).

Standing upside down on your forearms is hard. Being in love for a decade is harder. Watching a love story disintegrate is harder still. Raising a child in the process is the hardest. Best get some practice. We can form habits that deliver us, almost without us realizing it, to narcissism and self-destruction. And we can form habits that teach us to risk ourselves, to fall, and then to use our dorsal muscles to stand straight once again. The choice of which habits to actively cultivate and which emotions to feed may not be entirely up to us, but it is also not wholly beyond our control.

It is not surprising that James ends the *Principles* with a discussion of free will. In fact, in the course of three pages, he quickly recapitulates all of the arguments for determinism, the exact arguments that drove him into depression in his thirties. But not now. James was nearly fifty when the *Principles* was published, twelve years after he signed his contract, so arduous was the task. He had rejected determinism *in theory* many years before, but in the *Principles of Psychology*, he provided a practical manual for responding to the forces, like habit and emotion, that can impede and entrap us. In these cases, free will is required. "Freedom's first deed," he writes at the end of the *Principles*, "should be to affirm itself."[22] Its second and ongoing deed, at least for James, was to craft a practical, actionable plan to resist any encroachment on its liberty. James tried to stick to the plan, and occasionally succeeded. But a question remained: Do we have recourse when we fail?

4

Consciousness and Transcendence

Our life is always deeper than we know, is
always more divine than it seems, and hence
we are able to survive degradations and
despairs which otherwise must engulf us.
—Henry James Sr., *Christianity:*
The Logic of Creation, 1857

WILLIAM JAMES WROTE MUCH OF *The Principles of*
Psychology in a claustrophobic laboratory in the
Scientific School at Harvard: low-ceilinged, foul-
smelling, right-angled, austere, with little windows
that let in little light. He spent so many hours in the
lab during the mid-1870s, that it wasn't an over-
statement when he later claimed that empirical psychology in America had been founded in these small,
cramped rooms. Here, in extremely close quarters,
James got one of the first grasps on the neurological
basis of habit formation and human volition. It was
a strangely restrictive place to make sense of free

will, but he did his very best to explain how it worked and to describe its enabling and limiting conditions. James's reputation in the history of psychology as America's first cognitive scientist is hinged on this dutiful study. But this isn't exactly right. James's most radical insights about mental life arose when he ventured beyond the walls of the lab. Way beyond.

In the coming decade, James began to explore aspects of the human condition that he couldn't fully understand or describe, much less control. The motivations for this research were intellectual, but also deeply personal. He wanted to see if consciousness might allow him to transcend, or dramatically stretch, the bounds of human finitude. Perhaps you've had an experience that culminates in the thought, "Oh my God, that was *something else*!" James was on the hunt for just that "something," for that "else."

James's quest for the transcendent was motivated by the tragedies that quietly befell him in his forties. In 1884, his father died, and he spent much of this year collating and reviewing his father's writings on mysticism and theology in what became *The Literary Remains of Henry James*, which was, literally speaking, William James's first book. In the process of preparing these papers, James revisited his father's insight that

[e]very man who has reached even his intellectual teens begins to suspect that life is no farce; that it is not genteel comedy even; that it flowers and fructifies on the contrary out of the profoundest tragic depths of the essential dearth in which its subject's roots are plunged. The natural inheritance of everyone who is capable of spiritual life is an unsubdued forest where the wolf howls and the obscene bird of night chatters.[1]

Henry James Sr., however, believed that escape—spiritual and intellectual—was possible. Life can, despite the tragedy of it all, "flower and fructify." This belief was no small comfort to his son, who, on the heels of his father's death, lost his young son, Herman, whom James called Humster, to whooping cough that morphed into a fatal case of pneumonia. His father admitted that he had hardly gotten to know the child, leaving him to his mother, thinking that the son "would keep." Like all fragile, all-too-human things, Herman was kept only temporarily and then suddenly lost. The Jameses buried their boy in the corner of the family cemetery plot, in a coffin made of a wicker basket, in July of 1885. In his grief, James repeatedly wrote that little Herman had been "the flower of their flock" that had been plucked prematurely. The question was how life could go on, how could it "flower and fructify" again. The experience of losing Herman gave James "the taste of the intolerable mysteriousness of this thing called existence."[2] He couldn't will himself out of this situation. He couldn't habituate himself to this reality. Instead, James would go deeper into the mysteriousness of existence in order to see if it could be anything other than intolerable. His investigations of consciousness revealed that it could.

For the most part, James escaped personal tragedy by immersing himself in the writing of the *Psychology*, but, luckily, his meticulous bench research in the 1880s gave rise to an insight that there was something peculiar, and peculiarly awesome, about the workings of the human mind. His studies of consciousness bled, almost indiscernibly, into his desire for transcendence, and he discovered that the mind itself possessed redemptive potentialities. The deeper James went in his psychological studies, the more convinced he became that a full description of consciousness was unfathomable. Philosophy and psychology were to be experiential, but James would later state, "I firmly disbelieve, myself, that human experience is the highest form of experience extant in the universe."[3] According to James, any careful study of the mind would reveal that the dynamics and scope of experience always defied definitive explanation. There was always more to say, always simply more.

Empirical psychologists attempt to understand the mind by breaking it down, as one would cut apart an object, like a brain or spinal cord. The methods of empirical investigation just can't crack certain questions. For example, can we give an exhaustive explanation of the relationship between the mind and the body? Classically this question was called "the mind-body problem," but today, this specific question is called the "hard problem" of consciousness. In 1989, more than a hundred years after James researched the *Principles of Psychology*, the contemporary philosopher Colin McGinn wrote a paper in the journal *Mind* entitled "Can We Solve the Mind-Body Problem?" McGinn concludes in the negative. Consciousness is "a mystery that human intelligence will never unravel," and he argues that there is an insurmountable methodological obstacle: the objective method of science can only go so far in explaining the subjective experience of human beings. The felt "inside" of consciousness is something that scientific observations could never examine.[4]

James arrived at the same conclusion a century earlier, and for the same reasons. In "The Methods and Snares of Psychology," the seventh chapter of the

Principles, James writes, "To the psychologist . . . the minds he studies are objects, in a world of other objects."[5] In James's day and our own, psychologists study thought processes experimentally—as one might poke and prod a vivisected frog—by an empirical method that, in James's words, "taxes the patience to the utmost and could not have arisen in a country whose natives could be bored."[6] This method arose first in Germany, James continued, and here he found psychologists "bent on studying the elements of mental life, dissecting them out from the gross results from which they are embedded, and as far as possible reducing them to quantitative scales." This method is successful as far as it goes, but it doesn't really go that far, and certainly does not provide an exhaustive description of what most of us regard as "the mind." The reason for science's failure in studying human consciousness lies in its necessarily objective, analytic method.

James suggests that the problem with this method is that it forever misses the subjective sense of consciousness, the perspective of the "mind from within." And what James noticed when he attempted to conduct a "study of the mind from within" is that human thought can't be exhaustively described by laying it out on a dissection table, piecing it apart, and quantifying all the little bits. You do accomplish something when you do this: you destroy the very thing that you were intent on investigating, the lived experience of being human. In James's words from the *Principles*,

> The continuous flow of the mental stream is sacrificed, and in its place an atomism, a brickbat plan of construction, is preached, for the existence of which no good introspective grounds can be brought forward, and out of which presently grow all sorts of paradoxes and contradictions, the heritage of woe of students of the mind.[7]

If one's theory of mind runs counter to evidence and experience, it's best to consider altering the theory from the start. In contrast to the "brickbat plan of construction," in which the mind was composed of static, atomic pieces, James held that human thought was personal, continuous, and changing. Consciousness is not congeries of sensations that come, in Elbert Hubbard's words, "one damn thing after another." It also is not some thing of which one could be fully aware, as we sometimes refer to being "self-conscious." Instead it is a seamless movement, always in the middle of things—what James famously termed the "stream of consciousness."

Most contemporary philosophers regard James's proposal of the "stream of consciousness" as an intervention in the history of philosophy or the philosophy of mind. On this account, James is doing his best to undercut two arguments that had dominated modern philosophy for more than a century. First, he explicitly criticized John Locke's theory of "simple ideas," or unchanging mental facts that remain constant even in the flow of experience. Second, James challenged David Hume's notion that consciousness happens through the experience of what today is known as "sense-data," or a series of discrete mental images that appear directly to our perception. Yes, James was certainly engaging other philosophers. But to cordon off James's research into an academic debate doesn't do justice to his work on the "stream of consciousness" in the *Principles*. He was, in fact, setting the groundwork for a much more radical—and life-affirming—intellectual project.

The first proposition of the "Stream of Consciousness," according to James, is that thought is always personal, in other words, subjectively held and experienced. My thoughts are always at *my* disposal, to a greater or lesser extent. I have exclusive proprietary rights, so to speak, over my particular stretch of the stream. In James's words, "Each . . . [mind] . . . keeps its own thoughts to itself. There is no giving or bartering between them. No thought ever comes into direct sight of a thought in another personal consciousness than its own. Absolute insulation, irreducible pluralism, is the law."[8] Maybe you, like me, don't think your thoughts are particularly special, but James repeatedly argued that you'd be deeply mistaken about this. Thoughts are always perfectly unique and perfectly one's own. Everything can be taken from you, but you remain in possession of your stream of thought. Once your thoughts cease to be, well, so do you. James is once again channeling his transcendentalist inheritance, echoing Emerson's insistence that "Nothing is at last sacred but the integrity of your own mind."[9] What you do with your mind, what you notice, what you overlook are largely up to you. Let's begin there, James suggests: What exactly do you notice? Can you notice *more*?

Today my students use the expression that a person "is woke" to mean that one witnesses things that stereotypical thinking has made people miss. Somebody who "is woke," so I gather, is a person who has come to recognize the biases and prejudices of previous generations, and continues to grow of his or her own accord, with his or her eyes wide open. One sees life and oneself as he or she truly is. I tell my students I sort of get this. It's a bit like Thoreau at the end of *Walden* saying, "Only that day dawns to which we are awake. There is more day to dawn. The sun is but a morning star." They just shrug and say, "Yeah, whatever, the guy is woke." James's work on consciousness, from the outset, had this existential alertness, a type of Thoreauvian wakefulness, in view. He believed, following his transcendentalist forebears, that one of the saving graces of life was the ability to be conscious in the right way. Sure, most humans are conscious, but in James's words, "compared to what we ought to be, we are only half awake."[10] We sleepwalk through life, operating well below our experiential (and moral) thresholds. The chapter on the stream of consciousness in the *Principles of Psychology* is a preparatory step in rousing us. It sets the conditions for us to open our eyes, to be aware that the stream of consciousness is fast and wide and ceaseless in its flow.

Typically, I don't go with the flow. Instead, I have the tendency to get stuck in what David Foster Wallace calls my "own skull-sized kingdom," to get mired in and by my own mind. I assume I'm not unique in this, perhaps only peculiar in how early it occurred. When I was very young—five, perhaps—I'd often explain to my grandmother Hazel about how painful my day at school had been. I fixated on some real or imagined injustice that had affronted my kindergarten soul—and which now was keeping me from the blessed

oblivion of sleep that I so obviously needed and deserved. In the morning, when she'd waken me, she'd
always throw the curtains open, and, regardless of the
weather, proclaim it was a "pretty day." It was a possibility. But when darkness set in and my mood de-
scended, I forgot all about the possibilities and
brighter spots of the day, and I'd tell her how my waking hours had turned out to be altogether horrid. The
whole school was out to get *me*. She'd hold up a
gnarled finger until I was quiet: "You forget, John:
this too will pass. It already has," she would say. As a
child, I loathed this gnomic comment. It was only
slightly more palatable than her other favorite man-
tra, which was based on the same philosophical position. "John," she would say, "you can't step in the
river at the same place twice." This was the assurance
that any screwup or humiliation would not be repeated, at least not exactly. Tomorrow was another,
wholly different day.

Only very recently have I begun to recognize the
deep and abiding truth that my grandmother's comments expressed. This wasn't misplaced optimism or
wishful thinking. She was tapping into a basic fact of
the Jamesian stream of consciousness: this too shall
pass, indeed faster than we could ever think. It already
has. Any state of affairs, or more accurately, state of
mind, is temporary. In James's words, "*no state once*

gone can recur and be identical with what it was before."[11] We can, for example, hear exactly the same note played on the piano, but this sound is never the same one that we initially heard. Every experiential moment is one of delicate variation and subtle contrast.

In everyday life, I'm frequently in such a hurry that the transitory nature of the present is largely lost on me. The grass I see in my backyard is exactly the same green that it has always been. I fail to see the blues that drift and pass away around the roots, the purples that coat it in the evening, the off-whites that grace its blades on a dewy morning. "We take no heed, as a rule," James explains, "of the different way in which the same things look and sound and smell at different distances and under different circumstances."[12] Instead of attending to the pervasive differences between our experiences, we operate under the assumption of identity and similarity: this grass is the same as it was yesterday; this chore is the same as the one I did yesterday; this person will probably say the same thing she did yesterday. Sometimes life is easier this way. James, however, thinks that there is something deeply misguided about this rendering of experience. It may be easier, but not better. In the name of consistency we sacrifice particularity and possibility—and the beauty that they regularly afford.

Our stream of consciousness eddies, pools, and goes brackish.

This is not to suggest that consciousness can't settle, slow, and temporarily come to rest. It can, for a period of time. "Like a bird's life," James writes, "it seems to be made of an alternation of flights and perchings."[13] The perchings are the relatively stable moments of our waking life, when ideas solidify and take shape. But then it is off again. The rate of change may vary, but the bird remains on the move—unless we cage it or clip its wings. James explains, "When [its pace is] rapid, we are aware of a passage, a relation, a transition *from* it, or *between* it and something else. As we take, in fact, a general view of the wonderful stream of our consciousness, what strikes us first is this different pace of its parts."[14] James's description of consciousness is not a detached analysis. He calls it "wonderful" for a reason. Wonder—from the Old English *wundor*, meaning "a marvelous thing, a miracle, an object of great astonishment." James is drawing our attention to something remarkable but also remarkably easy to overlook.

For a long time, I didn't think that the "wonderful stream of consciousness" was that big of a deal. I just didn't get it: "So I don't notice the momentary differences of experience. So what?" But then I got older and discovered an aspect of adulthood that I'd never really considered—that one's middle years, even if they are objectively successful, are anything but wonderful. Instead, they can be alienating and humdrum. I was thirty-six when it really dawned on me. I thought I'd mastered James's will to believe and established some healthy-minded habits. But even after I willed myself through a divorce, a remarriage, and a series of existential U-turns, I still found myself, with growing frequency, dazed by the monotony and pained by a sense of disconnection. After starting a family, I really was doing better, even much better, which made this creeping uneasiness all the more disturbing. Like many people, I assumed that remarriage was going to permanently adjust my psychic life. Nope. Not a chance.

I didn't tell Carol. I didn't want her to worry. But she knew. I started doing more yoga, taking longer runs, and traveling by myself—searching for some activity that would be enjoyable. In the summer, I dragged the family to Switzerland in the hopes that I could find happiness in the Alps. Nothing. I went on medication. Went off medication. Went on medication again. What was wrong with me? I was either profoundly ungrateful or I was really messed up. Maybe both. David Foster Wallace, following James, said that each person has a choice about what to think and where to tap meaning. I should just try that, I thought. I would try to choose better things to occupy my mind. But this didn't always work, and I knew that DFW had hung himself by a shower rod when he was forty-six. I had a little less than a decade to figure this out. On some nights I wondered how much time I had left.

Today, three years later, when I go back to James's *Principles*, I am beginning to notice something that I routinely missed. Large swaths of the book are dedicated to the power of the will, the active element that can choose one action, one thought over another. There is, however, a certain antipodal tendency in the text—a desire to teach his readers not about activity, but rather receptivity. Be meaningfully active, but also passive and open at the right time, and more importantly, in the right way.

This sounds easier than it actually is. Our volition—and the practical pursuits that structure and organize our lives—is what keeps us from recognizing the full range of experience. We regularly confuse what is urgent and immediate with what is actually important or miraculous. Our habits, even the very good ones, close us off from what we might see and what we might become. "Blind and dead," James wrote, "does the clamor of our own practical interests make us to all other things."[15] His investigation of perception in the 1880s gave James an intimation that would later grow into full-fledged philosophical insight about the scope and meaning of consciousness:

> Most people live, whether physically, intellectually or morally, in a very restricted circle of their potential being. They make very small use of their possible consciousness, and of their soul's resources in general, much like a man who, out of his whole bodily organism, should get into a habit of using and moving only his little finger.[16]

James was right. I was still living in a very restricted circle. It was now, more or less, a circle of my own making, perhaps, but it was still carefully circumscribed. The goals and expectations of middle age—the hopes and fears that I had for myself and my loved ones—slowly warped the way that I understood, but more radically, perceived, the world. I'm not alone in this tunnel vision. James describes it as a failure to notice the living variation that underlies consciousness, the unreflective assumption that one instant of experience is exactly like the next, an inability to recognize the difference between and therefore the significance of things.

It is, however, possible to regain one's sight—slowly, or all at once. In a lecture James delivered in the early

1890s, he wrote, "This higher vision of an inner significance in what, until then, we had realized only in the dead external way, often comes over a person suddenly; and, when it does so, it makes an epoch in his history." This epoch-making moment isn't brought on or controlled by a clearly demarcated choice. It isn't simply a matter of choosing to change—as one might get a new job, or new partner, or new home. If it is a choice at all, the act of having "an experience" is something akin to the act of laughing: one might be more or less inclined and disposed, but it's never forced. We have the power to dull or preempt what James calls the "higher vision of inner significance," but cultivating and maintaining it is another matter entirely. For a person who is obsessed with the force of free will, who thinks that life's efficacy turns exclusively on one's decisions and practical activities, this discussion can be rather disturbing. It suggests that human meaning often depends on seeing things clearly as they appear and pass away, and that seeing things clearly means *not* acting and willing, but rather being quiet and still—in seeing something else. I was pretty good at forcing myself through sun salutations, but simply sitting, being present, and noticing things—well, that was much harder. James suggests that the "can do" mentality of the "Will to Believe" had to be tempered, in some cases quelled, with an experiential openness that the previous generation of transcendentalists had attempted to preserve. "As Emerson says," James writes, "there is a depth in those moments [of vision] that constrains us to ascribe more reality to them than to all other experiences. The passion of love will shake one like an explosion, or some act will awaken a remorseful compunction that hangs like a cloud over all one's later day."[17]

So how did William James, who spent much of his forties confined to a psychology laboratory, ever come to plumb the depths of this Emersonian transcendental experience? In truth, he had some help—a guide, a propaedeutic, and a proper setting. In 1874, Benjamin Blood published a thirty-seven-page pamphlet titled *The Anesthetic Revelation and the Gist of Philosophy*, which charted a course to the deepest, fastest-moving portions of the stream of consciousness. The experience of finding oneself, or—more accurately—transcending oneself, was Blood's ongoing fixation. And, beginning in 1860, he took extreme measures in its pursuit. He experimented with nitrous oxide—laughing gas or "whippets" (as the kids call it these days)—as a means of broadening, or breaking out of, his normal perception of reality. Blood wanted to write about the experience straight away, but waited for fourteen years, girding himself against the potential criticism, to publish *The Anesthetic Revelation and the Gist of Philosophy*. Blood explored the uncharted waters of consciousness, its flow and absolute depth: "After experiments ranging over nearly fourteen years," he wrote, "I affirm what any man may prove at will, that there is an invariable and reliable condition (or uncondition) ensuing about the instant of recall from anaesthetic stupor to sensible observation, or 'coming to,' IN WHICH THE GENIUS OF BEING IS REVEALED."[18] This was the first detailed description of a "trip" in America. And James would ultimately take his own journey.

In November of 1874, James reviewed *The Anesthetic Revelation*. Having just undergone his famous Renouvier experience, James experimented with freedom in all its forms, a path that ultimately led him to Benjamin Blood. "I forget how it fell into my hands," James would later write of Blood's account, "but it fascinated me so 'weirdly' that I am conscious of its having been one of the stepping-stones of my thinking ever since." This was slightly disingenuous: it fell into James's hands, no doubt, because he was interested in the same literally mind-blowing phenomena. When James reviewed Blood's testimony in the *Atlantic*, he wrote, "Now, although we are more than skeptical of the importance of Mr. Blood's so-called discovery, we shall not howl with the wolves or join the multitude in jeering at it. Nirvana, whether called by that name or not, has been conceived and represented as the consummation of life too often not to have some meaning."[19] James, even as a young man, was a scientist, and like any good scientist, he wanted to see Nirvana for himself. Over the next ten years, James followed Blood's lead repeatedly, testing different (even near-fatal) doses of nitrous oxide. It turned out that howling with the wolves might have been the appropriate response after all.

James and Blood shared a deep suspicion of the rational working and unthinking certainty of ordinary adult life. One can formulate, conceptualize, and argue, but what one produces in doing so is a sad substitute for what is most vital and meaningful: the sheer fullness and originality of reality. Now, with the help of laughing gas, James had proof: the real surpassed all formal comprehension. No human account could describe the experience—euphoric and horrific—of "coming to." Interestingly, his experiments with nitrous oxide gave rise not only to a critique of our everyday conception of reality, but also, and importantly for James, a warning against overblown philosophizing. Along these lines, Blood remarked that the "gist of all philosophy [is its] own insufficiency to comprehend or in any way state the All."[20] This is not to suggest that there is, in fact, an "All" that exists beyond the grasp of the human mind, an all-encompassing reality that could be gathered up as brickbat fragments into a perfectly unified whole. Rather, the experience of "tripping" indicated something quite different.

Summarizing Blood's insight, James explains that "[t]he secret of Being, in short, is not the dark immensity *beyond* knowledge, but at home, this side, beneath the feet, and *overlooked* by knowledge."[21] The "secret of Being" was, for James, revealed in the deceptively simple act of "coming to." In one sense, discovery is a matter of venturing physically and geographically elsewhere, but in another it is the act of waking up to what is always already present. It is sometimes the experience of stumbling onto something else, just beyond the scope of one's present attention, the feeling of "coming to": coming to consciousness, coming to a place, strange, slippery, but immediately present. This was the basis for a distinct form of mysticism, pluralistic rather than monistic in its focus, dynamic rather than static in its form. James, who was drawn to the mystical insight, but who eschewed the belief in some transcendent, all-controlling Absolute, would be hooked. James's ideas about consciousness were framed by his experience of "tripping" through the 1880s. His reading of Benjamin Blood created many of the "stepping stones" in his thinking. James chooses his words carefully: "stepping stone," like the type that helps you negotiate and explore a stream.

I can understand if exploring the stream of consciousness by way of psychedelics seems like a bad idea. Just because the eminently levelheaded Michael Pollan made exactly the same journey in his 2018 *How to Change Your Mind* doesn't mean that everyone is going to follow suit. Thankfully, for more timid readers like me, there are ways other than laughing gas to get a better sense of the stream of consciousness, to let go enough to feel a bit of release, to experience the flow rather than the fixity of experience. Sometimes simply attending to the edges and breaks of experience is enough to bring on a "coming to consciousness." Transcendent moments—whether you want to call them beautiful, or sublime, or genuinely divine—can occur after, or in the midst of great personal turmoil. It is as if something has been shaken free, the scales fall from our eyes, and we witness our surroundings as if for the first time. In truth, I suspect tragedy and turmoil have the unintended consequence of disrupting our habitual frames of perception, the instrumental ways that we typically interpret the world, just long enough for what James later called "pure experience" to make an entrance. Sometimes, it is precisely when one is laid low that momentary, but meaningful, insights have the chance to arise. "There is a crack in everything," wrote Leonard Cohen, "that is where the light gets in." And it gets in where you least expect it.

When my grandfather finally passed away, my small extended family gathered on a hill in a country cemetery in Exeter, Pennsylvania. It was August—humid and uncomfortable. We sat in silence for nearly twenty minutes "paying our respects." Becca, who was four at the time, had fallen asleep in the car and I held her on my lap, with her warm flesh pressed against my own. I wasn't crying because I missed Pop. He had Alzheimer's and had been a complete monster for the better half of a decade. I still don't know what the tears were, but they had to do with the little body, on top of mine, a onetime stranger who was now our lasting companion. This too would pass. The trees blew in the breeze and the water dripped off my nose into Becca's hair. My mother sat at my shoulder. The afternoon light smelled warm and green and yellow and passed into a cool blue that coated my eyes and covered my face. "Are you okay? Are you going to pass out?" my mother asked. I just shook my head and later explained that I thought I was "coming to."

In the year after my grandfather's funeral, I read Karl Ove Knausgaard's *Spring*. It is a brutally beautiful book, one in which tragedy occasionally gives way to what might be regarded as conversion of consciousness. In the lingering months of winter, Knausgaard's wife overdoses on sleeping pills, and he narrowly (and haphazardly) saves her. But the months pass, and he writes,

> Some days in spring it is as if the landscape here opens up in every direction, in the weeks before all the green unfolds in earnest, when the trees are still naked and the ground is still bare as if it were winter, while the sun shines with the fullness of summer and the light meets no obstacles, isn't bound up by the cornfields or the grass, the canopies of the trees or any of the other growing things which, as soon as they are here, create little pockets around themselves and become places in their own right. On such days in spring the landscape here seems placeless, and the volume of air beneath the sky, through which the light falls, is enormous.[22]

These miraculous days usually occur without our taking note, our attention and volition devoted to other, seemingly more pressing matters like work or kids or friendship or marriage. It is only in the sudden suspension of these activities that we discover something that has always been there: the enormity of the volume of air beneath the sky or light as it falls and meets no obstacle. This openness can be caused by a crack, but no matter. It is openness nonetheless and, for James, no less important than the free will that we exercise in the pursuit of a meaningful life. How similar is Knausgaard's description of spring and James's attempt to articulate the "beginning of coming to" in the *Principles* in which "one has at a certain moment a vague, limitless, infinite feeling—a sense of *existence in general*."[23]

"A sense of existence in general" is not "grasped," or comprehended (which literally means the same thing), or scrutinized (which means sorted out), or "gotten." It frustrates our typical means of understanding. There are, however, books that testify to its meaning and reality. In the twentieth-century American culture, there is one that stands out, a book that the grandfather of modern religious studies, Huston Smith, called "the most Taoist Western book I know— Thoreau's Walden not excepted." This is Henry Bugbee's *Inward Morning: A Philosophical Exploration in Journal Form*. Bugbee, inspired by James and Thoreau, was never just your average philosopher. He got his doctorate at Princeton and went to teach at Harvard in the 1950s, but he didn't fit in: Bugbee was interested in experience rather than rigorous analysis.

Had he written and taught at Harvard in the late nineteenth century—like James—he might have led the department and the discipline, but as it was, he was forced to leave the Ivy League and spent his years in the intellectual hinterlands at the University of Montana.

The Inward Morning, which takes its title from Thoreau's description of being "woke," is the most personal of philosophical reflections, a series of journal entries that shows how the immersive experiences of a young man could come to support a philosophical life. James's work on the stream of consciousness in the *Principles* points to the dynamic reach of experience and beckons us to enter. Bugbee tells his reader what it is like to slip into its waters. During his days at prep school, Bugbee explains that winter would slowly break, and when it did, so did the water in the swamps behind the school. It was time to go "swamping." He writes,

> Moving about in the swamp, sometimes you would find ice, questionable ice that almost wouldn't hold you . . . the grassy clumps would be fairly solid and you could always begin with the intention of keeping dry . . . even when there was no ice and the mounds were a bit soggy you would never just wade in. But no matter how sure your leaping was, there

was always a clump a little too far off for which you would try, or a clump would roll . . . there was something about the water in the swamps that made it impossible to stay out. . . . Once thoroughly in, the acknowledgement would come over you that it couldn't be otherwise, and you would abandon yourself to the swamp, water and all. How deep could the water get?[24]

Bugbee, following James, understood that when the will fails us—when you "abandon yourself to the swamp"—it may be enough to simply be awake and to notice the dawning of things. He admits that this experience was not "particularly pleasant." It wasn't like watching Netflix or playing on your iPhone, but Bugbee holds that "there was no mistake about the gladness of being in the swamp or the immanence of the wilderness there."[25]

Our lives don't necessarily have to break or shatter in order for water and light to get in, in order for us to receive what James called "the higher vision of inner significance," but the desire to see life anew is, as Henry James Sr. observed, often heightened by despondency and crisis. There is a gladness in deep waters. It is impossible not to reach, as far as one can, for the bottom or the surface. And darkness has its virtues—it can force us to actually use our eyes.

In 1885, after his father and son passed away in a matter of months, William James responded by retreating to a newly purchased tract of land in the White Mountains of New Hampshire, in the small town of Chocorua. James's house is a beautiful one—clapboard, gabled, cedar-shingled—but its owner spent most of his time on the surrounding woodland, or sometimes literally in it. The house was in the middle of a level meadow. James wanted it to be on a hill, to have the appearance and vantage of being up high. So he moved several tons of earth to make it so. Most of the environs of Chocorua, however, can't be remade. One can only hope to experience them: the cone of Mt. Chocorua, at 3,500 feet; the lake at its base that stretches for miles; the spring between them that connects elevation and depth. This was a place, untamed and untapped, where the mysteriousness of existence could stretch the bounds of consciousness. In such a setting, consciousness can grow.

"What I *crave* most," James wrote of his trips to Chocorua, "is some wild American country. It is a curious organic-feeling need."[26] What exactly was this need? James suggests that it is a certain proclivity for open spaces. The impulse for possibility yet realized. Charles Sanders Peirce, echoing Emerson, once wrote that "experience is our only teacher," and in Emerson's words, "life is a series of surprises."[27] Exposure to wild country, like the far reaches of the White Mountains, can *bewilder* us, but perhaps this feeling of thoroughgoing puzzlement also makes us better students of experience and attunes us to the faintest surprises.[28] Experience isn't static. It is never monotonous, monochromatic, monovalent, or monolithic. It only seems that way when we fail to notice what is happening at its borders and in its flux. James wrote that their house in Chocorua had "fourteen doors, all opening outwards." Outwards—that is where James's study of consciousness was directed.

"Experience itself, taken at large, can grow by its edges," James maintained in the *Principles*. "That one moment of it proliferates into the next by transitions which, whether conjunctive or disjunctive, continue the experiential tissue, can not, I contend, be denied. Life is in the transitions as much as in the terms connected."[29] Having spent time in the rural border country of Chocorua, James writes of the growing edge of consciousness that is "like the thin line of flame advancing across the dry autumnal field which the farmer proceeds to burn."[30] The flame is the moving point of transition, a frontier where past and future, death and rebirth, meet for the time being. This is the present moment where life takes place and we neglect it at our greatest peril.

This might all be true, but in the world of money and power and fame, the value of the present moment makes very little sense: it can't be commodified, or packaged, or viewed on a screen. You can't deposit it somewhere safe or save it for a rainy day. James holds that the transitions of consciousness are valuable precisely to the extent that they suck us into the flow and frustrate any attempt to constrain them. They are precious *because* they pass away so quickly. In his studies of consciousness, in his losing a child and father, in his woodland explorations, James discovered what Emerson had described in his seminal essay "Experience," namely "the evanescence and lubricity of all objects which lets them slip from our fingers when we clutch hardest."[31] Sometimes it is best, therefore, not to clutch at all, but to stand close, to be "in it," and to witness. In James's copy of the *Principles of Psychology*, in the margins of a section of text that addresses the slipperiness of the stream of consciousness, he scrawled a single phrase: "The Witness."[32] The witness isn't the willful overseer who wants to determine the outcome of an event, but the witness also isn't just any bystander who simply stands by to look. The witness is detached yet involved, engaged in a purposeless purpose: to carefully testify to the unfolding of things as one sees them.

There is a sort of koan-like quality to speaking of the stream of consciousness, and I know better than to think that I am going to sort it all out. I have struggled for decades to explain this to my students. Sometimes I give up and just point to an experience had or undergone. But, on the whole, I do not agree with Wittgenstein that "What we cannot speak about [with perfect accuracy] we must pass over in silence." So I will continue to struggle. Success happens in degrees. I hope there can be value, even life-and-death value, in partially failed attempts. The stream of consciousness is arguably James's greatest contribution to philosophy, but not for the reasons that are often discussed by contemporary philosophers. James suggested, persistently in his later writings, that immersing oneself in the stream, and orienting ourselves to its mystery, could bolster or, in some cases, save a life. Sometimes simply witnessing how the world lives and moves might be reason enough to stay alive.

None of this is to say that stable ideas—the truths we live by—can't arise in the stream of consciousness. James, however, suggests that the act of "conception," of conceiving discrete thoughts in the midst of the perceptual flow, is usually performed as a kind of hindsight. One looks back on where one has floated, or swum, or swamped in consciousness, and then attempts to make sense of the circuitous journey. The singularity of the trip is compromised in the description, but the hope is that our concepts about our world, our habits of thought, help us negotiate and control it. The danger is in allowing these descriptions—even our most beautiful and cherished stories—to stand in for experience, and thereby mask the transitions where life, according to James, happens.

5

Truth and Consequences

We have to live today by the truth we can get
today and be ready tomorrow to call it
falsehood.

—William James, "The Conception of
Truth," 1907

ALL THOUGHTS ARE, AT FIRST, afterthoughts. They
arise after the fact. The formation of a formal philosophical school is similarly born in retrospect: it
comes into being as a way of describing what has
come and gone in an intellectual community, sometimes for a very long time. Today, William James is
known in philosophical circles as the founder of pragmatism, arguably the only distinctively American
school of philosophy. I have, to this point, been relatively silent on this particular claim to fame. This has
been intentional: foregrounding pragmatism in our
story would have, in my grandfather's words, "turned
everything bass akwards." James did not, from the
start, have pragmatism in view as a philosophical

tradition. Instead, he slowly, thoughtfully, sometimes gropingly, made his way through early adulthood. Even his groping, however, was deeply meaningful, the stuff that can, I think, save a life or make soul a little less sick: his struggle with determinism, his excavation of free will, his emphasis on action and habit formation, his sensitive study of the stream of consciousness. These were the different vectors of meaning that helped James make it to middle age. Yes, pragmatism happened on the way, but it appeared so gradually that its formation actually took James by surprise at the beginning of the twentieth century. By that time, James was already living by a worldview that attempted to combine a respect for scientific fact with a desire for something more. The public articulation of this worldview as "pragmatism" was largely an afterthought. When James died in 1910, his friend, neighbor, and colleague Josiah Royce remarked, "I am sure that James himself was very little conscious that he was indeed an especially representative American philosopher. He certainly had no ambition to vaunt himself as such."[1]

There is another reason not to concentrate too fanatically on the importance of pragmatism in James's corpus. These days pragmatism is usually regarded as a distinct position in epistemology, in other words, as a particular theory about the nature of truth and belief. And it is. What is often overlooked, however, is that pragmatism is also an existential and normative stance regarding the relationship between truth and human meaning. James would formulate the pragmatic maxim in many ways over the course of his career, but it boiled down to his claim that truth in ideas is their power to work.[2] He realized that this statement highlighting the practical function of truth drew a number of questions in its wake: How does truth work? Why does it work? For whom does it work, and for how long? And what is the meaning and worth of this work? To embrace the pragmatic theory of truth is at once a commitment to become more, much more, than a formal epistemologist, one who theorizes about knowledge.

We should remember what James is after: something people actually crave in their daily lives. "*You* want," James suspected, "a system that will combine . . . the scientific loyalty to facts and willingness to take account of them, the spirit of adaptation and accommodation, in short, but *also* the old confidence in human values and the resultant spontaneity, whether of the religious or of the romantic type."[3] The pragmatic theory of truth demands that one respect, always, the force of empirical fact, but also realize that all facts lead or point to consequences, the meaning of which cannot be exhaustively evaluated in a scientist's lab. We are to think through the enduring goods—both moral and aesthetic—that give the consequences of truth their purchase. To be a pragmatist, in the Jamesian vein, is therefore always to become a student of life's value and worth, and this is not exactly the same as being a "student of philosophy." As a professional philosopher, I often have trouble remembering this point, restated so often by James, that "[p]hilosophy lives in words, but truth and fact well up into our lives in ways that exceed verbal formulation."[4] This comment, one that is meant to curtail philosophy's delusions of grandeur, is at the very core of James's thought, and his pragmatism should not be removed from this frame. At the outset of *Pragmatism*, a slim, but surprisingly dense book published in 1908, which provides a set of variations on pragmatism, James warns his reader how simple, yet how deleterious, it is to divorce philosophy from the realities of life. He writes of a recent student (maybe William Ernest Hocking, maybe his colleague Josiah Royce), who came from a "western college," whose final thesis dramatically reflected this potential problem:

[The student] began by saying that he had always taken for granted that when you entered a philosophic class-room you had to open relations with a universe entirely distinct from the one you left behind you in the street. The two were supposed, he said, to have so little to do with each other, that you could not possibly occupy your mind with them at the same time. The world of concrete personal experiences to which the street belongs is multitudinous beyond imagination, tangled, muddy, painful and perplexed. The world to which your philosophy-professor introduces you is simple, clean and noble. The contradictions of real life are absent from it. Its architecture is classic. Principles of reason trace its outlines, logical necessities cement its parts. Purity and dignity are what it most expresses. It is a kind of marble temple shining on a hill.

In point of fact it is far less an account of this actual world than a clear addition built upon it, a classic sanctuary in which the rationalist fancy may take refuge from the intolerably confused and gothic character which mere facts present. It is no EXPLA-NATION of our concrete universe, it is another thing altogether, a substitute for it, a remedy, a way of escape.[5]

Pragmatism is not a means of escape. When I suggest that William James's philosophy might save a life, I'm not suggesting that he will rescue you from it. In my experience, on good days, it can return one refreshed and undaunted. "Be not afraid of life," James reminds us. Pragmatism is not a marble temple on a hill that can only be reached by abandoning the lowlands of human existence. Pragmatism is a structure, but we are already inside. James occasionally called it a hallway that leads to a number of different doors: they are unlocked, but you get to pick which ones you wish to open. It is a method, not a destination—a way, not an end point. I like to think of it as a home, not unlike James's house in Chocorua, with many windows and doors. The windows provide specific, but expansive, lookouts. The doors open to pathways that lead God knows where. This is not a place of worship, built of marble, but a place to dwell and meet the world. At times, the point of pragmatism might be to transcend it.

Philosophically speaking, James attempted something very hard, maybe impossible, at least for one person. He wanted to craft a philosophy that was absolutely honest to the twisted, often contradictory, facts of life, but also to the desire that many of us have to transcend them. In his words, he wanted to provide a way of thinking between the "tough-minded" scientist and the "tender-minded" idealist, preserving what is valuable about both sides.

A tough-minded thinker, such as the British empiricist David Hume, maintains persistent and radical doubt regarding the prospects of human knowledge. "You want truth?" the tough-mind says. "Well, good luck. You'll never achieve one iota of certainty. The empirical evidence is always changing and therefore always against you." This was too tough for James. The tender-minded philosopher, epitomized by systematic thinkers such as Gottfried Leibniz, on the other hand, holds that truth is secured and guaranteed by some superhuman force or cosmic system. "You want truth?" they retorted. "You're in luck. God already has that figured out for you. You're good to go." This wasn't nearly tough enough for James.

The pragmatic theory of truth does not embrace absolute skepticism regarding the prospects for a certain type of veracity, but it is not "simple, clean and noble" like the pretensions to absolute Truth. The inherent messiness of pragmatism is not a deficiency of James's thinking, but rather a function of his desire to mediate between these two extreme epistemic positions. Pragmatism remains tangled, muddy, painful, and perplexed, because life itself is tangled, muddy, painful, and perplexed. But pragmatism is also hopeful because life often warrants it. It is a philosophy for humans like us, who are neither rocks, hopeless objects devoid of reason, nor gods, exalted beings imbued with omniscience. So let us not pretend we are worse or better off than we actually are. We are born into a uniquely compromised position—somewhere *between* amoebas and angels—but we have the chance to work through it. James seems to echo Emerson's insistence in "Experience" that this "mid-world is best."[6] If we were amoebas or angels, there would be pitifully little to do, and there certainly wouldn't be anything such as success.

Perhaps this middle-of-the-road philosophy seems a bit unsatisfying. Many of us want more from our philosophers. We want them to be more-than-human— to figure out our lives for good, to give us all the answers, to keep us perfectly safe. I once had a friend who suddenly veered into evangelical Christianity (this too is a type of philosophy with a very understandable appeal), and when she was confronted with tragedy or confusion she'd say, "This makes sense. It really does. Everything makes sense—just not to you or me." She was implying that some sort of Divine force had our lives sorted out, even if we felt wholly wrecked. However, that was little comfort to me. Hers was precisely the deterministic stance that James spent most of his life rejecting, one that ran counter to the desire to live in a world in which one's own thoughts, opinions, and actions actually mattered. My religious friend was secure in her faith, but what had she relinquished in exchange for that? James suspected that the "rationalistic" impulse to create a model of the universe that was completely tidy, logically consistent, and divinely governed could only be satisfied if one were also willing to lose touch with reality.

James refused to lose touch. He was, from beginning to end, committed to experimentation, and, along with Peirce, identified the pragmatic method with what most people now consider the modern scientific method of hypothesizing, prediction, and empirical testing. The facts may be out there, waiting for us to find them, but the truth is our story *about* the facts, and it is not "out there," like a quarry that one hunts down and then holds for all time. Indeed, truth isn't even an attribute of reality, something that could be objectively ascertained and perfectly copied. Truth is an attribute *of our ideas*, and, as one of James's closest students, Ralph Barton Perry, noted, it "attaches to ideas in proportion as they prove useful for the purpose for which they are invoked."[7] In James's words, "Truth happens to an idea. It becomes true, is made true by events. Its verity is in fact an event, a process: the process namely of its verifying itself, its verification. Its validity is the process of its valid-ation."[8]

It would be foolhardy or arrogant to expect perfect fidelity between the facts and our understanding of them. The truths that we live by today hopefully correspond to reality in some way, but this is rarely a one-to-one correspondence. Another way of saying this is that truth is a matter of representation, an account of reality, rather than perfect reproduction. Ideas hardly ever remake the facts of the sensible world. They are abstractions, or signs, tethered to the world in a variety of ways. A map schematizes a landscape, presenting only the likenesses of geographic facts that might orient a traveler. A traffic sign indicates a factual state of affairs, one that has passed away, one that remains, or one that will come into being. A painting stems from and elicits the fact of fleeting feelings. A poem speaks to some aspect of a landscape, a fact that defies our attempts to explain it. A song reflects the rhythm of life, its syncopated beauty and tragedy. All of these are representations, and all of them are accountable to facts, albeit in different ways, and all of them can "succeed" in a practical sense of the word, and all of them can be true depending on how they work.

Two years ago, at the end of a lecture on pragmatism, one of my very good students raised her hand: "So you're saying that all my ideas are true because I find them useful? Because I think they're working well *right now*? So pragmatism is just relativism. Right?" She gave me a concerned look. This was a question that worried James deeply. The response wasn't going to be an easy one. I took a second and then leaned gingerly into an answer: "Well, not exactly. Ideas should be judged on the basis of their practical consequences, but this is not the same as saying that whatever is useful at a particular time, for a particular person, is necessarily true. This isn't just the 'will to believe' where you can make the truth happen in the absence of factual support. Facts matter." She nodded hesitantly. Manipulative statements, hidden betrayals, seamless lies, fallacious ideologies—all of these aim to be extremely useful and enjoyable (for particular parties at particular times) despite being pointedly devious. James knew this: truth is not simply whatever is expedient.

My student, however, had asked the right question, and James was regularly at pains to guard against relativism—what the ancients would have called "sophistry"—the position that truth is simply a function of the specific interests of individuals or their community at any given time. In 1885, James published "The Function of Cognition," an essay that he later claimed was "the *fons et origo* [source and origin] of my pragmatism,"[9] in which he outlined the central tenets of the pragmatic theory of truth, which can be read as a response to my student's concern.

James opens the essay by identifying truth with the success of ideas. This success, however, is not determined at one time, by one person, in a single practical situation. Instead, an idea succeeds, literally "moves forward," through many tests, conducted by many different people, over an extended period of time. It is like science in this respect. The success of any specific inference is validated only for the time being in a provisional fashion. Ultimately, *complete* success, capital-T Truth, would be achieved only in the infinite long run; in other words, it is not the sort of certainty that we should expect in our lifetimes. At best, we can hope to negotiate life by way of little-t truths, which guide us more or less successfully in our daily affairs. These certainties, however, are always necessarily modest. In James's words, "We have to live today by the truth we can get today and be ready tomorrow to call it falsehood."[10] This sort of epistemic humility is entailed by James's insistence that the consequences of our ideas must be accountable and lead back to the sensible world of experience.

In many cases, James suggested we can falsify ideas, make relatively accurate predictions, answer questions, and reach agreement, by simply being faithful to the facts—realities that repel or reinforce our ideas. Ignoring these realities, or dismissing their interpretation as "fake news," is to give up on the pragmatic method altogether. Truth happens to ideas only through the ongoing and collective conversation with sensations, moments in the stream of consciousness that either sustain them, wash them clean, or wash them away. In James's words, "[S]ensations are the motherearth, the anchorage, the stable rock, the first and last limits, the *terminus a quo* and the *terminus ad quem* of the mind. To find sensational *termini* should be our aim with all our higher thought."[11] At these points, our ideas are tested against experience: Do the predictions stipulated by our theories coincide with the world that we sense or feel? Or are our representations of the facts out of whack with experience? The answer usually is sudden and obvious, for, James remarks, "sensations destroy the false conceit of knowledge." He is not saying that sensations destroy all claims of knowledge, only its false conceit. What is left, after the dust settles, is a representation or idea better equipped to handle the facts of life.

Evaluating the success of ideas is not confined to the laboratory, or, if it is, it is enacted in the great, very unsterile, laboratory of the world. It took me a long time—I was in my thirties—before I really understood the life-and-death significance of the pragmatic method of testing ideas against experience. When Carol and I decided to have children, we did what any two bookish parents would do: we went on Amazon, bought a truckload of books, and read all about it. According to the experts, we were supposed to practice hypno-birthing and believe in natural childbirth; we were supposed to breast-feed till the child was two because formula was poison; we were supposed to use cloth diapers; we were supposed to feed the child homemade organic solids because store-bought was poison; we were supposed to wear the child at all times in any number of easy-to-assemble slings; we were supposed to sleep train the child—otherwise we'd be sharing our bed until he or she was an adolescent—but we were also not supposed to sleep train, because it was tantamount to child abuse; we were supposed to co-sleep with the child, but we were also not supposed to, because co-sleeping was tantamount to child endangerment; we were supposed to clothe the child in homespun organic shirts and pants because store-bought contained poison; we were supposed to allow the toddler to run around naked for as long as possible. After all of my reading and studying, I thought I had a pretty good sense of this parenting thing. I was ready. But Carol was two weeks over term. She was going to be induced tomorrow. Tomorrow came. The induction happened. Tomorrow went. Then we waited for two more days—in the hospital.

By the time the baby finally arrived, Carol was so full of Pitocin that Becca basically popped out, like a balloon that has been inflated very slowly to an unsustainable point. In all of my reading, I'd somehow missed that babies could swallow the amniotic fluid on their way out. Sorry. I know it's gross. For some mysterious reason, Becca wasn't hungry or happy when she greeted the world. She wouldn't "latch" on to Carol, who, after several hours, passed her over to me, and got some needed sleep. I sat in the adjacent room with a squalling infant, who eventually spit up that gross stuff in her stomach—all over her father. But she kept crying because she was now, at long last, hungry. I asked the nurse for a bottle. Of course, like any good medical professional, the woman protested: this was exactly the time to give Becca back to her mother. I assured her that this was exactly the time to give me a damn bottle. She did, and Becca never breast-fed. Not once. And, by the way, cloth diapers didn't work for us either. Neither did the perfect parity of co-parenting or perfect egalitarianism. Some things can't be taught in a book.

My first adventures in parenting wouldn't have surprised James at all. In my careful study of childrearing, I'd formed a stable picture of what it was supposed to be like. This stable picture was what the Romans might have called a fixed (*stereo-*) form (*tupos*): a stereotype. It turned out that this stereotype couldn't accommodate, or help me negotiate, the actual experience of being a father. I know I could've acted differently. I could have tried to force experience to conform to my preconceptions, but at a certain point, this "pushing the river" is obviously futile. I could have read more books or thought about the situation in a more rigorous fashion, but James might have reminded me that this would probably amount to rearranging the preconceptions that I already possessed.

Sometimes it is best to let experience have its say, and reform one's theories on the basis of what is actually said. This is what James is encouraging us to do in "finding sensational *termini*," experiential end points at which our ideas can either succeed or fail. According to James, there is another advantage in tethering one's ideas to the ground of experience. Experience is *common* ground—the place where individuals with different ideas can meet and, many times, reach agreement. In order to evaluate any two theories, one is to look to their respective practical consequences and trace out their "sensational *termini*." If they reach the same end points, the ideas can be said to be practically the same. This goes for ideas that seem to be quite divergent in theory. They should be checked—in practice—in order to distinguish any real or meaningful difference.

Carol and I, like most parents—and definitely like most divorced couples—don't always see eye to eye about how to raise our child. This is a euphemistic way of saying that we argue about it—fight like hell, really. I'm sure this will continue beyond the foreseeable future. Philosophers have the ability to battle tooth and nail about a host of ideas that don't really matter. Just imagine what happens, then, when two philosophers think a beautiful child's entire future rests in the balance of a single disagreement. It's not pretty. Over the years, and even through divorce, however, we have learned something from James, who at the end of "The Function of Cognition" suggests that many arguments are "like fighting with the air; they have no practical issue of a sensational kind."[12] He is right: many of our arguments can be traced to conflicting stereotypes rather than any practical difference of opinion. So Becca doesn't say "thank you" every time she is handed something. Should Carol and I argue about it? Or should we drill down into the experience of living with our daughter: Is she turning into a generally grateful child or a monstrous little tyrant? We can try to answer this question together, in moments of careful attention to the concrete realities right in front of us. If we ignore these shifting experiential realities, James wrote, "we are all at sea with each other's meaning."[13] Without recourse to common experience, it is only a matter of time until two people talk past each other and, in dramatic cases, reach incommensurable positions.

Now, in our pragmatically minded moments, Carol and I manage to put a lid on our argument (at least until the next day or week), to co-parent our child so that we can share the experience and, hopefully, reach some semblance of agreement about what is actually going on. It often turns out that the situation has changed overnight, and it's suddenly possible to avoid the fight that seemed almost destined to happen the night before. This isn't just a matter of cooling down, but also simply paying attention. If we attend to facts of experience, nothing is destined. Something else is always possible. We surprise ourselves to find that we were, all along, free to cooperate, and that the world, unexpectedly, affords us the chance. When this happens, we don't create a more perfect union (that would be totally impossible at this point), but rather something just a little better and more honest than the stereotype of divorced parenting. To be clear: we are not especially good at this. We are just trying.

James's defense of free will hovers in the background in the pragmatic theory of truth as an assurance this change is possible. It is up to us. Embracing free will is the first step in affirming optimism about our ability to adapt and grow in the face of life's challenges. "Meliorism," James's term for this hopeful worldview, does not insist that improvement is inevitable, but that it is still quite possible. In *Pragmatism*, he writes,

> Free-will pragmatically means NOVELTIES IN THE
> WORLD, the right to expect that in its deepest ele-
> ments as well as in its surface phenomena, the future
> may not identically repeat and imitate the past. That
> imitation en masse is there, who can deny? The gen-
> eral "uniformity of nature" is presupposed by every
> lesser law. But nature may be only approximately uni-
> form; and persons in whom knowledge of the
> world's past has bred pessimism (or doubts as to the
> world's good character, which become certainties if
> that character be supposed eternally fixed) may nat-
> urally welcome free-will as a MELIORISTIC doc-
> trine. It holds up improvement as at least possible;
> whereas determinism assures us that our whole no-
> tion of possibility is born of human ignorance, and
> that necessity and impossibility between them rule the
> destinies of the world.[14]

Obviously, we could both be mistaken about our
parenting strategies—hard questions always remain
partially open—but a pragmatist might suggest this
indeterminacy is a necessary part of figuring things
out together. We are both wading through the weeds of
co-parenting in divorce, trying our level best to make
our way. I'm not sure, but when Carol and I occasion-

ally manage to experience Becca's world together, I suspect James would be proud of us. I am absolutely sure that our lives improve when we remain responsive to the changing facts of our daughter's life, when our minds meet in the thick of it, so to speak. That is the truth as I see it, and one that I am not yet ready to dismiss.

Pragmatism is about life and its amelioration. That's it. And that is enough. What could matter more than this? Other than this? James was interested in "the truth" only to the extent that the modest certainties that we live by might lead to the improvement of our not-so-easy-to-endure condition. This was clear to James even in the very best of times. After publishing the *Principles of Psychology* in 1890, he became an academic superstar and could have easily coasted to the end of his career by revising what almost immediately became a classic textbook in empirical psychology—but he didn't. Instead he used his reputation, and the invitations that it garnered, to embark on two decades of amelioration. It was in these two decades William James became a pragmatist.

How did James improve the world? Mostly by talking to—and teaching—its inhabitants. He was a brilliant writer, but, according to his students, an even better teacher. Between 1893 and 1899, James gave dozens of large public lectures across the country: from Chautauqua in upstate New York, to Hot Springs in the middle of Virginia, to Colorado Springs, to Berkeley. When I say large public lectures, I mean hundreds of people would regularly travel, in a time when traveling was not altogether easy, to hear James speak. He was occasionally invited to lecture exclusively on the *Principles*, but much more often was asked to address general political concerns, social ills, and moral crises. In James's age, there was still something noble about a philosopher being a public intellectual. That time would quickly pass as the discipline of philosophy relegated itself to the ivory tower in the twentieth century, but James was spared witnessing the full extent of its self-marginalization. In the second half of his career, James became a philosopher, the value of which turned on his practical effects. He wanted, sometimes rather desperately, for his thoughts to matter.

By the 1890s, James's life as a social and political reformer was unified by a coherent philosophical worldview espousing the sanctity of personal freedom, the respect for individual difference, the primacy of meaningful action, and an attentiveness to the experiential realities of individuals and their communities. James spoke repeatedly against imperialism, which he viewed as an affront to freedom; drunkenness, which he viewed as a self-inflicted "handicap" to action and thought; against the bureaucratization of education, which reduced wisdom to calculable metrics; and against racism and lynching, which were reflections of a latent and brutal mobbishness in our thinking. These weren't pet causes for James, the kind of sporadic activism that comes into vogue and fades away, and they weren't, as Royce later remarked, merely "incidental" to his formal philosophical writings. He rejected "bigness" in all its forms—institutions and ideas that had grown too big for their britches, that were bloated, that reflected the arrogance or hubris of their makers. James witnessed the growth of big government and big business with something akin to horror: "Damn great empires!" were his words in response to Roosevelt's expansionist policies at the turn of the century.[15] "Bigness" ignored the sometimes humble, but always vitally important, potentialities of human individuals. Big institutions tended to treat individuals as mere parts, and not particularly important ones. Big ideas tended to understand people and experiences as types or tokens of a single unifying category, regardless of the many ways in which they might not perfectly fit. In the face of "bigness," individuals were either used or simply absorbed.

Given James's rejection of "bigness," it wouldn't make any sense for his experience of teaching to take place in "big," impersonal lecture halls. It didn't. James's pedagogy at Harvard was pointedly "small"— neatly tailored to the lived experience of his students. He repeatedly taught Philosophy D, by many standards the most popular course that had ever been taught at the university. It was popular for good reason. James's pragmatism insisted that philosophy could still have life-and-death significance, and Philosophy D addressed an array of existentially loaded topics, the kind that many academics assiduously avoid: truth, freedom, God, evil, suffering, death, and the meaning of life. This was not some dry Power-Point presentation or truth-table exercise. "The man of genius," Emerson tells us, "inspires us with a boundless confidence in our own powers."[16] This is what James aimed to do in lecturing and writing philosophy: to encourage his students to wrestle with life's most difficult questions. And to do so—bravely— on their own terms. But this didn't mean that students were just left to fend for themselves. Far from it. James was unusually close to his pupils and one of the few Harvard professors who would respond to questions from the floor during his lectures. His students, unsurprisingly, loved the intellectual and emotional intimacy that his classes provided. James encouraged young adults to cultivate their own powers, and he regularly criticized colleagues who seemed more intent on gathering acolytes or perfect replicas of themselves than fostering the unique talents of each student.

In 1899, James collected and edited a series of lectures that he had delivered to teachers and students in Cambridge seven years earlier. These *Talks to Teachers* amounted to the CliffsNotes version of the *Principles* and were, to James's mind, deadly boring. The last three chapters of the book, however, entitled "Talks to Students"—those, according to their author, were actually worth something. These lessons are on "some of life's ideals" and give a clear picture of the existential and ethical message that the mature James painted for his students in his "smaller" classes.

The first of these lectures, "The Gospel of Relaxation," delivered to the members of a female gymnasium in Cambridge, drilled down into the "*Binnenleben*," or "the buried life," of an increasing number of students whom James regarded as "unhealthy-minded."[17] To be clear, James wasn't judging or shaming these young women. He identified with them, and, ultimately, tried to improve their lives. The *Binnenleben* of the "unhealthy-minded, apart from all sorts of old regrets, ambitions checked by shames and aspirations obstructed by timidities, it consists mainly of bodily discomforts not distinctly localized by the sufferer, but breeding a general self-mistrust and sense that things are not as they should be with him (or her)."[18] This self-mistrust may often be a reflection of certain biological or psychological predispositions, but James was not about to resign himself (or his students) to the fates of one's neurological makeup. The sense of dis-ease experienced by a sufferer might begin in a predisposition, but it frequently grows and is cultivated in a particular setting that James wanted his listeners to confront.

For many people, especially women of James's day and our own, the experience of being "sick-souled" is a reflection of being penned in by the explicit or tacit expectations of their surroundings. In this case, adjusting one's *Binnenleben*—"the unuttered inner atmosphere in which his consciousness dwells alone with the secrets of its prison-house"—is not accomplished by an act of introspection, but rather a novel attempt at extroversion.[19] Something must be done. James's suggestion is clear: form good habits that stretch, and in many instances break, societal conventions. He highlighted cases like the Norwegian women who took up skiing and physical activity, deviating radically from current cultural scripts, and thereby escaping the stereotype of the "sedentary fireside tabby-cat."[20] Obviously not everyone can, or wants to, go skiing, but James suspects that on the fringe, or growing edge, of consciousness each of us can imagine acting in ways that might invigorate, rather than dampen or mute, our lives. Take a look at the fringe. See what is there and, more importantly, why it's there instead of being enacted at the center of things. What forces are keeping it at the periphery? Society hums along smoothly by virtue of conformity, but its maintenance is often secured at the expense of individuals whose unique prospects are sacrificed. The imperative to act freely, for the mature James, was coupled with an explicit critique of the social structure that forbade it. "The need of feeling responsible all the livelong day has been preached long enough in our New England," James wrote in conclusion. "Long enough exclusively, at any rate—and long enough to the female sex."[21] Breaking the societal mold often looks irresponsible, to the extent that it violates certain mores or duties, but this sort of transgression is often a means of becoming the author of one's life, and that, James suggested, may be the true meaning of responsibility.

James strove for authenticity and praised it in his students, even when it led them to neglect their duties. Gertrude Stein was one of these students. She once had to sit for James's examination and found herself completely uninterested in doing so. So Stein didn't. Instead, at the top of her exam, she wrote, "Dear Professor James, I am so sorry, but really I do not feel a bit like an examination paper in philosophy today." She just wasn't "feeling it," so she got up and walked out. The next day, James posted his student a short note: "Dear Miss Stein, I understand perfectly how you feel. I often feel like that myself."[22] And then he gave her a high mark in the class. The whole point of teaching is to inspire individuals to exercise their minds and wills in all sorts of unconventional ways. Stein's grade, according to James, was well deserved: she had followed what it is often difficult or forbidden to acknowledge, namely what one actually feels.

For James, moral rectitude is not keyed to our ability to follow the rules. Instead, being responsible is an issue of coming to terms with one's actions and, even when they are unflattering, owning up to them. Yes, the responsible person is accountable to the standards of his or her community, but James argues that we are ultimately accountable to ourselves, to the inner sense of significance that arises (or doesn't) in a particular activity. "Do my actions have the feeling of the 'real me,' or am I just half-asleep, play acting at the only life I have?" This is the question that plagued James in early adulthood, but it steadily became the working pivot in his moral outlook. In "A Certain

Blindness in Human Beings," the second essay in his "Talks to Students," he wrote that meaning is found

> [w]herever a process of life communicates an eager-
> ness to him who lives it, there the life becomes genu-
> inely significant. Sometimes the eagerness is more knit
> up with the motor activities, sometimes with the
> perceptions, sometimes with the imagination, some-
> times with reflective thought. But, wherever it is
> found, there is the zest, the tingle, the excitement of
> reality; and there is "importance" in the only real
> and positive sense in which importance ever any-
> where can be.[23]

Zest: a word with an unknown root, the feeling of a keen passion. For James, this was the key to human meaning, "ever anywhere." When my sick soul strug-gles, it is, I think, because I can't find, or generate, or even feign, the zest. James is right that it can be found everywhere—in activity, perception, imagination, or reflection—which, I have to say, is little comfort when I can't find it anywhere. In these moments, I often make like "Miss Stein," and identify what I find most zest-less, so to speak, what leaves me feeling wholly numb or empty. And then I try *not* to do that. In the Middle Ages, theologians discovered the *via negativa*, the "negative way" of reaching God; they outlined the Divine by articulating what it is not. When I can't find the "zest" in any given activity, I take a similar route by avoiding the activities I find particularly deadening. Thankfully, this *via negativa* gets me through the days, and often delivers me, after some time, to a zestful experience.

I'll try to be honest: when I finally experience the "zest," it comes as such a welcome relief that I tend to cling to it with the white-knuckled fury of a desperate man. If the zest is embodied in another person, I spend every waking moment with my new friend or lover. If the zest is found in a sport, I will destroy my body at its service. If the zest appears in writing or reading, I hardly sleep. Zest is just that intoxicating and all-consuming. I am overly invested, indeed downright possessive, when it comes to the zest. James was similarly impelled, but he came to see the drawback of doggedly pursuing our keen passions, and it isn't just that zest almost always fades. It has to do with the zest experienced by others, and our inability to recognize it. Concentrating on one's own intensely meaningful experiences has a tendency to produce what James called a "certain blindness in human beings":

Each [of us] is bound to feel intensely the importance of his [or her] own duties and the significance of the situations that call these forth. But this feeling is in each of us a vital secret, for sympathy with which we

vainly look to others. The others are too much absorbed in their own vital secrets to take an interest in
ours. Hence the stupidity and injustice of our opinions, so far as they deal with the significance of alien
lives. Hence the falsity of our judgments, so far as
they presume to decide in an absolute way on the
value of other persons' conditions or ideals.[24]

Zest is the vibrant "inside" of human meaning, but
with the seductions of this vibrancy lies the danger of
getting lost inside our own point of view. It's too easy
to forget that other people's inner lives—their joys
and sorrows, their hopes and disappointments—are
every bit as immediate and real to them as ours are
to us. When we notice strangers at all, it is often as if
through the window of a slow-moving car: we drive
by, we rubberneck, we gawk, but for the most part
strangers are the sorts of things to be avoided. This
misanthropy is rooted in a very basic self-centeredness,
a narcissism so deep and ubiquitous that it seems
altogether normal.[25] We are meaning-making creatures, but, for the most part, we are only concerned
about the meanings that each of us individually makes.
Perhaps we extend care to our immediate circle of
friends and loved ones, but that is about it. The rest
of the world is "beyond us," at least in the sense of
genuine recognition.

In "On a Certain Blindness," James admitted that he had long suffered from this shortsightedness. On a trip to North Carolina, James explained, he traveled through a rural shantytown in the mountains and could find absolutely nothing beautiful, or noble, or meaningful about it. The place just looked dead. No zest at all. He wanted to get out as quickly as possible. As he did, however, James had a thought that gave him pause, one that has often slowed me down in the frantic pursuit of my own zestful experiences. Is it not possible, even quite likely, that the men and women who live here, their children and their pets, all live lives that strive after similar moments of meaning? Is it not possible, that they long for and find zest in their surroundings in precisely the way that I do? Yes, it is possible.

Now let's be careful here. James wasn't saying that the strangers whom we see through a glass darkly have the same experiences that we do, that we should project our own wants and desires on the people we pass on the street or in the market. He was precisely not saying this. He is suggesting that individuals tap meaning—and experience zest—in singularly unique ways. In other words, we are the same precisely because there is an irreducible difference between the zests that make our worlds meaningful. And, at the same time, the disappointment and tragedy of zest-unrealized or zest-extinguished is a similar feeling of utter alienation and loneliness. *We feel ourselves apart in the same way.*

In the history of moral theory, ethical communities usually consist of members who share common loyalties or characteristics. Maybe they worship the same God or flag. Maybe they all possess reason and this gives them incomparable worth. Maybe they all can experience pain and pleasure. There are, however, individuals who are uncommon—who don't worship the "right" things or exhibit the "right" attributes. These deviant individuals aren't granted access to the communities in question. In truth, they are usually treated like outcasts. Communities based on commonality can be surprisingly exclusive.

James, like Arthur Schopenhauer nearly a century earlier, was after an ethical community based on difference. Schopenhauer claimed that individuals were "companions in misery."[26] Suffering "individuates," meaning it is experienced subjectively, in isolation, but this, in fact, is the underlying commonality of the social world. Each of us suffers in our own unique hellholes, according to Schopenhauer, but this is the isolating fact that each of us shares. We don't suffer exactly the same miseries, ever, but this difference should be enough to engender a bit of compassion for those around us.

James, I think, is making a similar philosophical move: the fact that each living being makes meaning in its own perfectly unique way, that zest, when it arises at all, arises *on the inside* first and foremost, this is the belief that connects a Jamesian community without dissolving the individualism he held dear. James wants to respect difference and individual variation from beginning to end. This is more than what philosophers call "the no-harm principle," namely the idea that my freedom ends at the tip of your nose, that I don't have moral permission to harm you with my liberty. James, following Schopenhauer, has genuine acceptance in view. He closes "On a Certain Blindness" with an admonishment:

And now what is the result of all these considerations and quotations? It is negative in one sense, but positive in another. It absolutely forbids us to be forward in pronouncing on the meaninglessness of forms of existence other than our own; and it commands us to tolerate, respect, and indulge those whom we see harmlessly interested and happy in their own ways, however unintelligible these may be to us. Hands off: neither the whole of truth nor the whole of good is revealed to any single observer, although each observer gains a partial superiority of insight from the peculiar position in which he stands. Even prisons and sick-rooms have their special revelations. It is enough to ask of each of us that he should be faithful to his own opportunities and make the most of his own blessings, without presuming to regulate the rest of the vast field.[27]

This "vast field" of reality continually outstrips our attempts to understand it. No story can capture the whole of life. No one, not even God, can make complete sense of it. In 1897, James's friend Benjamin Blood wrote that he believed "in only lower-case gods, and in no climacteric results of being." This was James's belief as well, that, in Blood's words, "everything happens in the middle of eternity."[28] Eternity affords many truths, instead of a single overarching Truth. And whatever is true, even in the slightest way, has consequences that make it true, and these consequences matter whether they impact the house I call home or a prison or sickroom I will never visit. My refusal to consider this consists, according to James, in a failure of insight and imagination. His suggestion is rather simple: try harder.

From the top of William James Hall, everything seems very distant. But with a set of binoculars, you can almost look into the second-floor window of the hall, which was constructed near the end of James's career at Harvard and today houses the Philosophy Department. At the center of the department is Robbins Library, a semiprivate, semisecure collection of books used by faculty, graduate students, and philosophy majors. And at the center of the library stood a strange but unassuming object. When I found it in 2011, it had remained untouched for more than a century. At one point, it was tucked on the top of a bookcase in the back of Robbins: ten inches tall, cast in pewter, the perfect drinking chalice for a Harvard undergraduate.

The engraving on the cup has faded but is still quite legible: "To Professor William James, with Reverence and Admiration from his last class in Philosophy, Harvard University, January 22, 1907."[29] On this winter evening, James, who was by then widely regarded as the master teacher of Harvard's campus, gave his last lecture as a professor to a packed hall at Emerson. At the end of his career, he routinely remarked that the university was slowly changing, and not for the better. It was time to get out. It was becoming too "big." In 1903, he'd written an essay in the *Harvard Monthly* called "The Ph.D. Octopus," a satirical but disturbingly prescient take on the future of higher education. He prophesized that our universities would be partitioned by the professional cliques of departments, and defined by the hyperspecialization that only a cliquish culture can beget. Teachers—the kind who might entertain meaningful questions about the meaning of life—would be replaced by "Professors," experts in the art of professing ever more rarified jargon. And loving cups would be replaced by peer-reviewed articles.[30]

If you take a careful look at the loving cup, you'll notice that the students of Philosophy D commissioned another line of inscription beneath the dedication. One of the few complete fragments from the ancient Greek philosopher, Protagoras: "Πάντον χρημάτων μέτρων άνθρωπος" (Man is the measure of all things). James had a long and, what I take to be, ambivalent relationship with this fragment. Most scholars take Protagoras to be advocating a type of skeptical relativism—that each of us has access only to our own perceptions, and therefore truth and reality are in the eye of the beholder. The correlate usually follows: there is no objective or absolute truth. James, along with his philosophical colleague, F. C. S. Schiller, had certain sympathies with this position. In the words of James from "On a Certain Blindness," "neither the whole of truth nor the whole of good is revealed to any single observer, although each observer gains a partial superiority of insight from the peculiar position in which he stands."[31] There is, for the pragmatist, no such thing as a view from nowhere, some elevated position from which to evaluate truth claims. Rather, all claims are made in the thick of things, in the specific contexts of what John Dewey (pragmatism's representative at the University of Chicago and Columbia University) would later call "problematic situations." From beginning to end, philosophy was to be experiential: it was done in the midst of experience and judged on its ability to interpret and enrich it.

James sympathized with Protagoras's skepticism, but he spent his later years defending pragmatism against claims that it was a philosophy without a moral or epistemic backbone. Critics like Bertrand Russell would repeatedly argue that pragmatism was a crass instrumentalism that tipped too easily into an "anything goes" worldview that prioritized efficiency above all other values. The last years of James's life were spent guarding the pragmatic maxim against a growing number of critics who thought it was a license to confuse the immediately beneficial with the permanent goods of life. In *Pragmatism*, however, James explained that the practical consequences by which truths were verified were never local and provincial, but rather emergent, distant, and yet to be determined. One might need to act on the truths on hand at a given time, but to do so was an act of hope. The verdict was still out on a wide array of truths, but until the verdict was in, one could live on. James maintained that a philosophy could be skeptical about the prospects for objective truth and logical abstraction without producing a vicious relativism.

Like Protagoras, James suggested that our access to the absolute was always partial, usually pitifully so, and so he was skeptical about any grand claims about its nature and meaning. James, however, did not foreclose the possibility that men and women could carry on, often triumphantly, in the face of uncertainty. His students, like Stein, W. E. B. Du Bois, e. e. cummings, Horace Kallen, and William Ernest Hocking, admired James's realism about the human condition, but were also inspired by their teacher's belief that this condition could be expanded or, better yet, transcended, at least for the time being. For a Jamesian, Protagoras lays down an existential gauntlet: Can you live like you are the measurer of all things? Can you live like the life of the universe depends on it? These are the questions of a committed humanist, one who holds that the meaning of life is up to the liver. You can act on a whim. Go ahead. Just know that you must always own up to your actions. If "man" is indeed the measure of all things, individuals must be prepared to shoulder absolute responsibility.

I am convinced that the inscription on James's loving cup speaks to a radical humanism that risks being lost in today's culture. I am also convinced that it points to another, more hidden, meaning that may be lost on many of the students who study in Robbins. Emerson Hall opened its doors at the end of 1905. Its construction was the physical manifestation of philosophy's professionalization. The building and the educational enterprise were going to be big business. Henceforth, philosophy, and Harvard's psychology laboratory, would have their own building on campus, separated off from the other academic disciplines. Departments and intellectual canons would grow independently, never the twain to meet again. As philosophy grew more insular in the twentieth century, it would jeopardize its own significance. James predicted this and, I suspect, saw Emerson Hall as a sign of the prophecy's fulfillment. So James didn't exactly care for Emerson's construction, but he did concern himself with one aspect of the new building: the inscription that was to be carved over the front entrance. A committee of philosophy faculty, led by James and George Herbert Palmer, proposed a number of possible phrases and finally settled on one: "Man is the measure of all things." James sent the decision to Harvard's president, Charles Eliot, and the scaffolds went up for the carving to be completed.

Charles Eliot was a Harvard institution—a true "big" man. He'd been appointed in 1869, at the tender age of thirty-five. One of his first acts as president was to appoint James as a lecturer in physiology. The debt that James owed Eliot, however, did little to mask their divergent views of education. Eliot had been James's chemistry teacher. And James hated chemistry. It was boring and practical in all the wrong ways—instrumental, formulaic, tedious. Sort of like many of the administrators who came to dominate higher education in the late nineteenth century. Eliot was one of them. He was a businessman and a bureaucrat. A relatively nice one, a surprisingly progressive one, but still a bureaucrat. He oversaw the transformation of Harvard from a small college, to a national university, to a world-famous research institution. He made Harvard into a financial behemoth and frequently played with the idea of purchasing the little school down the street called the Massachusetts Institute of Technology. James admitted that Eliot's "economic powers were first rate," but complained that the president had "great personal defects, tactlessness, meddlesome, and disposition to cherish petty grudges."[32] To a man like Eliot, James's forays into a variety of academic fields—biology, psychology, philosophy, religion—must have seemed highly inefficient. The existential fervor that James brought to his classroom probably struck Eliot as extravagant or simply useless.

So when Eliot received the recommendation from the inscription committee, he did what any administrator would do—he ignored it. Instead of broadcasting the controversial humanism of Protagoras, Emerson Hall would be graced with a question from the book of Psalms: "What is man that thou art mindful of him?" This was an echo from Harvard's strict Calvinist past, perhaps a reminder to the Philosophy Department (or James) not to get too uppity. Calvin explains what we should glean from this particular passage from the Bible. And it's not that human beings are the measure of all things. On the contrary, Calvin writes,

> We see that miserable men, in moving upon the earth, are mingled with the vilest creatures; and, therefore, God, with very good reason, might despise them and reckon them of no account if he were to stand upon the consideration of his own greatness or dignity. The prophet . . . [implies] that God's wonderful goodness is displayed the more brightly in that so glorious a

Creator, whose majesty shines resplendently in the heavens, graciously condescends to adorn a creature so miserable and vile as man.[33]

Eliot was not a particularly devout man. But he, like his Calvinist predecessors, worshipped order and disdained individual opportunity. Salvation was not achieved through a person's effort or intellect or force of will. Instead, it was a function of some impersonal design that had nothing to do with nobodies like us. The best that we can do is resign ourselves to the Divine plan. And be grateful. James could not have disagreed more strongly. And he spent his career fashioning pragmatism in protest.

The loving cup, presented a year after the façade of Emerson Hall was unveiled, was, for James, a consolation prize. Eliot could dictate what went on the buildings of his university, but he was unable to determine exactly what went on between students and their beloved teachers: human beings, their lives and their meanings, were still the measure of all things. And that is, for teachers who remain committed to James's style of teaching, a very good thing. On my more jaded days, I think that the loving cup, tucked away in a room in Emerson Hall, is left alone because the discipline of philosophy—or more frightening, our culture—no longer cares about teaching or about the human experience. But in my more hopeful moments in which I feel the truth of James's meliorism, I can come to another conclusion. Perhaps the loving cup and James's pragmatic conclusions are safe because they are, by their very nature, inviolable.

6

Wonder and Hope

The greatest use of life is to spend it on
something that will outlast it.
—William James, quoted by Perry in
Life and Thought, 1935

TWO YEARS AGO, ON A LATE AFTERNOON in October, I
decided to walk from my hotel in Manhattan to
Brooklyn's Community Bookstore. It was a cool day,
on the cusp of evening, at a moment when things,
even grimy New-York-type-of things, seem to glow,
and I was so busy looking around that I almost didn't
notice the small white sign at the bottom of Brooklyn Bridge. The green lettering was newly painted and
read, "LIFE IS WORTH LIVING."

For many people, life's worth is never in question.
It never becomes a topic of conversation or debate.
Life is simply lived until it is not. But something bothered me that day, and continues to hound me: If life's
worth is so obvious, why was the sign put up in the
first place? It is, I know, because there are those who

occasionally find themselves on the top of the bridge, contemplating a quick and fatal trip to the bottom. Decades after battling depression in 1870, James wrote to Benjamin Blood that "no man is educated who has never dallied with the thought of suicide."[1]

To my surprise and delight, the walkways on the bridge were empty. I'd have the view to myself. With a maximum height of 276 feet, it was once regarded as one of the seven wonders of the industrial world. Twenty workers died in the construction of the bridge, which was completed in 1883. The first man to jump, not fall, was Robert Odlum, who wanted to prove that descending through air at high speed was not necessarily fatal. He died. In the next century, approximately 1,500 people have followed Odlum. Every fifteen days another jumper takes his or her life in the East River. I'm not sure how many people the sign saves, but I am inclined to think it's pitifully few.[2]

It was chilly at the top. I looked across to the Statue of Liberty in the harbor and then back into Manhattan where William James had grown up. Then I looked down. There was a terrifying liberty in this—the choice to live and die in a particular moment as time stretches out endlessly in either direction. After reading James for most of my adult life, this liberty still has its appeal. I think it always will. Pragmatism might save your life, but never once and for all. This is a

philosophy that remains attuned to experiences, attitudes, things, and events, even when they are the tragic
ones. While James occasionally disparaged Arthur
Schopenhauer's pessimism (he refused to give a cent
to a memorial in honor of the German philosopher),
James's posthumous writings reveal a deep respect for
the grim thinker's willingness to stare clear-eyed into
the gloom of human existence. There was something
like courage in this brutal confrontation with quickly
impending darkness.

According to James, the sign at the bottom of the
bridge should be repainted or at least amended: LIFE
IS WORTH LIVING—*MAYBE*. In 1895 he explained
to a crowd of young men from the Cambridge YMCA
that "it depends on the liver."[3] It is up to each of us
to, literally, make "what we will" of life. These days,
when I peer down from great heights, in addition to
experiencing vertigo, I almost always think about Steven Rose, the young black man who threw himself
off William James Hall in 2014.[4] Perhaps James's
"maybe" could have saved him—the suggestion that
he was still in charge of his life, that the decision to
end it all might be reasonable, even respectable, but
so too was the possibility to live. The possibility was
right there—still, always, even in the shit and rancor
of it—for him to explore. Perhaps he thought that
choosing to die was the only free decision at his

disposal, but James always suggested there might be other options.

For the majority of people, free will can be exercised in any number of ways, which don't have to include committing suicide, and in many of these cases one can choose to embody new habits of thought and action. This is the case, even when all is lost. If meaningful freedom seems evasive or unrealistic, most of us still have a choice about what to see and what to look past. This too can be worthwhile. "The art of being wise," James suggested, "was knowing what to overlook."[5] Maybe these possibilities could have kept Steven Rose alive for even longer than they did. Maybe not. I refuse to presume.

I think one surefire way to send jumpers off the edge is to pretend that you know something they don't: that life has unconditional value and that they are missing something that is so patently obvious. On the ledge, I suspect they'd detect some deep insecurity or hubris in this assertion. And they might jump just to prove you wrong. Because you would, in fact, be wrong. In James's final entreaty in "On a Certain Blindness," he reminded his readers that they often don't have a clue about how other people experience the meaning of their lives. Better to leave it at "maybe."

I looked across the water as the sun skimmed the cityscape. Night would fall and a million stars would once again compete with a million electric lights. In the short term, the electric lights would probably win. In the indefinite long term, the stars almost certainly would. Between these poles, it was anybody's guess. For now, I believe that James's "maybe"—the open question of life's worth—is right, or at least right for me, because it maps my existential situation as one who is not always entirely sold on life's value. It is also right, I think, because his "maybe" is roughly fitted to the open question of the cosmos. Everything, from smallest eukaryotic being to the most complex organic system, is in the process of making its own guesses, the first protological step in what we humans call "inferences." Without good guesswork there would be nothing like adaptation or growth, and, for us, there would be nothing like meaning. James followed Peirce in believing that the world is teeming with hypotheses, with the "maybes" that make life, in all its many forms, possible, and make our lives worthwhile. For James, stars do not burn, much less appear, in perfect order, and human lives are not settled in advance. As Emerson wrote in his poem "Circles," one of James's favorites: "let me remind the reader that I am only an experimenter."[6] The "maybe" remains constant, or as constant as a "maybe" can be. This is for the best: it gives us something to watch and expect and experience. Persistent variation gives rise to persistent wonder, and, for James, this sense of mystery—of chance—was often enough to see him through when other practical measures failed him. "No fact in human nature is more characteristic," the mature James asserted in the *Varieties of Religious Experience*, "than its willingness to live on a chance. The existence of the chance makes the difference . . . between a life of which the keynote is resignation and a life of which the keynote is hope."[7]

If you throw something off a bridge into the water below, it breaks the surface and is immediately gone. Just G-O-N-E, a four-letter word of finality, like "dead" or "fate" or "lost." There's no chance of getting it back or preserving it, no matter how desperately you might try. Over the years, I've often imagined what it would be like to lose something precious in deep water, something far more precious than one's keys or iPhone. For small material objects, I suspect that there is little hope of preserving anything. And I have entertained the possibility that this is the case with everything: keys, iPhones, wallets, relationships, and lives. Maybe everything just departs without a trace. Some philosophers would be perfectly happy with this explanation—that everything is in the process of passing away, that at the end of the cosmic day, nothing will be left. I am just not one of these philosophers. Neither was William James. The certainty of this fatalism runs counter to James's "maybe" and counter to a hope that is, for me, hard to live without.

Take an object—a small rock or an your phone—to a shallow river. Throw it in. On a still evening, the ripples are still moving, still growing, when the object comes to rest on the bottom. The disruption at the point of entry is the first to vanish, but the consequences of the event radiate concentrically even as they dissipate. In a narrow river, with steep banks, the waves strike the shore, recoil to the center and make for the opposite side. The small perturbations are real regardless of our ability to feel them. Something is left.

"Our life is an apprenticeship to the truth, that around every circle another can be drawn," Emerson explains in "Circles."[8] Fifty years after the poem was published, James finished the *Principles of Psychology*, in which he developed a model of selfhood that resembled radiating spheres. At the center was the "material self," our bodies and material fortunes. This is frequently regarded as the most concrete aspect of our lives, but it is also, according to James, the most superficial. We typically would be willing to give up our material fortunes for the subsequent ring, what he terms "the social self," the recognition that one gets from friends, family, and loved ones. Finally, James explains, there is the "spiritual self," one that is sought or experienced in "intellectual, moral, and religious aspiration."[9] This is the most expansive aspect of self-hood, the farthest reaching, but also, for many of us, the most subtle and easily neglected. This is the wave that matters even when it is not fully detected or articulated.

In the last decade of James's life, he began to argue that while man may be the measure of all things, there may be a reality that exceeds all measure. Philosophy was to be experiential, but he claimed in 1907 that "I firmly disbelieve, myself, that human experience is the highest form of experience extant in the universe."[10] The waves ripple out, strike the opposite shore, and make their way back—gently. Occasionally we feel them. On rare occasions they are all we feel. It is a remarkable person, according to James, who can sense them deeply with any regularity. It is this type of unique individual that occupied much of his attention when he developed the 1901 Gifford Lectures in Natural Theology at the University of Edinburgh, a series of talks that became the *Varieties of Religious Experience*, published in the subsequent year.

James was never a churchgoing man. For the most part, he wasn't interested in institutional religion or the doctrinal aspects of the spiritual self. He was, as always, interested in experience and life, and in his final years he began to turn explicitly to thinking through the religious possibilities of both. He refused to limit these possibilities, insisting in the *Varieties*, "Were one asked to characterize the life of religion in the broadest and most general terms possible, one might say that it consists of the belief that there is an unseen order, and our supreme good lies in harmoniously adjusting ourselves thereto."[11] This adjustment to the unseen order could take many forms and was never restricted to a particular church, temple, or mosque. Indeed, James looked for it everywhere leading up to the writing of the *Varieties*. His exploration into the unseen carried him into experiments with psychotropic drugs but also into a spiritual realm that modernity often dismisses as mere quackery; today, if something cannot be seen with perfect clarity, it seems easiest to assert that it cannot be seen at all.

When his aged father and fledgling son died within a year, James and his wife Alice tried to contact them: in September, James visited Leonora Piper, a medium who had become a Boston sensation for supposedly channeling spirits. He had his doubts about Piper but concluded that the woman might have what he called "supernormal powers."[12] James was still, and always, the consummate empiricist, and wanted to test these powers more carefully. Luckily there was a fledgling organization dedicated to precisely this study—because James created it. The American Society for Psychical Research was founded in Boston in 1885. Its mission was to investigate all things "supernormal." This was not some nut-job organization, but it was not altogether normal, either. One of its founders, G. Stanley Hall, had come to Harvard to do doctoral work with James in the late 1870s and was awarded the first psychology degree in the United States. With James's support, Hall organized a group of researchers to explore the possibility of things like spirit contact, divining rods, and telepathy. They spent thousands (I do not exaggerate this number) of hours interviewing mystics and séance sitters. By 1890, Hall had resigned from the organization, concluding that parapsychology amounted to pseudoscience. But others, like James and his close friend the physician Henry P. Bowditch, marshaled on into the turn of the century. In 1909, James reflected on twenty-five years of ghostbusting:

At times I have been tempted to believe that the Creator has eternally intended this department of nature to remain baffling, to prompt our curiosities and hopes and suspicions, all in equal measure, so that although ghosts and clairvoyances and raps and messages from spirits are always seeming to exist and can never be fully explained away, they also can never be susceptible of full corroboration.[13]

Nature loves to hide. Humans, like James, love to seek. Despite the bafflement—or perhaps because of it—James and his fellow researchers remained pointedly, if cautiously, hopeful. Unlike most psychics of the time, however, the members of the psychical-research society documented and published their findings. None of those were anywhere near conclusive, but they did help to push the boundaries of science, to explore an area that science couldn't quite explain. This record became the *Journal of the Society for Psychical Research*, for members and close associates, and the *Proceedings*, intended for the general public. I'm always surprised by the sheer magnitude of the volumes: a little more than ten thousand pages in total. Somewhere between curiosity and suspicion was abiding hope.

When James began his psychical research, he was well ensconced in the field of physiology. The anatomist's factual, objective method, however, missed something crucial in its understanding of human nature. For James, something important was lost: the sense that a human being is more than just a bundle of perceptions and nervous reactions, and more than just a body that could disappear without a trace. He hoped that there was something ethereal, transcendent—something even ghostly—that was free from the constraints of our physical lives. And at many times throughout his life, he suggested that one can occasionally feel this "something" haunting the fringe of consciousness. As late as 1901, James remarked that "I seriously believe that the general problem of the subliminal . . . promises to be one of the great problems, possibly even the greatest problem, of psychology."[14] "Subliminal" is often used interchangeably with "unconscious," but it shouldn't be. It refers, instead, to mental processes just below the threshold of consciousness that can often be felt without fully emerging. Just a hint, a fleeting "maybe," is all we get, but it is often enough to qualify as something that we know, at least for a moment. These glancing blows of experience stand at the center of James's *Varieties*—they come in many forms, indeed so many that their existence cannot be pushed aside. Oliver Wendell Holmes once joked that James would turn down the lights in a room so that the miracles could happen. I think there is some truth in this. James was definitely always ready and willing to experience the unseen. When you turn the lights down, your pupils dilate so that more light can get in. I can't blame James for this. Maybe we surprise ourselves with what we can see.

And maybe that is miracle enough. For secular skeptics, this might be as far as they are ever willing to go when it comes to religious experience: to dwell deeply, to "live a little" in the present. In the *Varieties*, however, James goes just a little farther, a little deeper.

Sometimes, when you turn the lights very low, you can see things more clearly. James describes such a phenomenon, one that he claimed could only be described as genuinely "mystical." Recounting the "hour of rapture" of a clergyman, James writes in the *Varieties*, "[t]he perfect stillness of the night was thrilled by a more solemn silence. The darkness held a presence that was all the more felt because it was not seen. I could not any more have doubted that HE was there than that I was. Indeed, I felt myself to be, if possible, the less real of the two."[15] The "HE," according to the clergyman, was undoubtedly the Judeo-Christian God, but what we call this presence scarcely mattered to James. "He" is a very old word, older than gender and sex, meaning "this here." "This here" was present all the more felt because it wasn't seen. For James, for his fellow mystics like Benjamin Blood, there was a sustained comfort in this story. "We are," as the German mystic Novalis wrote, "more closely connected to the invisible than to the visible."[16] This too is a possibility, and the Jamesian pragmatist is happy to entertain it.

In James's day, before the Brooklyn Bridge was
built, a ferry carried passengers from one side of the
river to the other. Walt Whitman was often among
the crowd. Whitman was one of James's long-
standing heroes, the embodiment of the capacious
"healthy-mind" he describes in the *Varieties*. James
occasionally sensed the sublime or the religious on
his hikes in the Adirondacks or in the testament of
mystics, but Whitman could tap into it on a routine
basis, even on a dirty ferry ride, which most people
would regard as a rather annoying commute. It
wasn't annoying for Whitman. In his "Crossing
Brooklyn Ferry" from *Leaves of Grass*, he wrote of
the spectacle—the experience of nature and the experience of the human throng. Both were inexpli-
cable and hopeful and shared:

> Others will enter the gates of the ferry, and cross from
>   shore to shore;
> Others will watch the run of the flood-tide;
> Others will see the shipping of Manhattan north and
>   west, and the heights of Brooklyn to the south
>   and east;
> Others will see the islands large and small;

Fifty years hence, others will see them as they cross,
the sun half an hour high.
A hundred years hence, or ever so many hundred years
hence, others will see them,
Will enjoy the sunset, the pouring in of the flood-tide,
the falling back to the sea of the ebb-tide.
It avails not, neither time or place-distance avails
not.[17]

James read and reread this poem. This was wonder, and there was enough to go around. Whitman's vision, in James's words, was sufficient "to prompt our curiosities and hopes and suspicions."[18] The world is not always, or ever, exactly as it seems. A dirty ferry ride may be more than just a dirty ferry ride. There is something more—at least it is possible. Whitman's was a type of religious experience—and so very different from the way that most people experience the world. Reflecting on "Crossing Brooklyn Ferry," James explains,

> When your ordinary Brooklynite or New Yorker, leading a life replete with too much luxury, or tired and careworn, about his personal affairs, crosses the ferry or goes up Broadway, his fancy does not thus "soar away into the colors of the sunset" as did Whitman's, nor does he inwardly realize at all the indisputable fact that this world never did anywhere or at

any time contain more of essential divinity, or of eternal meaning, than is embodied in the fields of vision over which his eyes so carelessly pass.[19]

One does not have to be careless, however. Thankfully there are other ways to pass the time and other times to pass away. The flood and the ebb continue to go out and come in. And James suggests that it is possible, even for a pragmatist, to occasionally feel the reassuring cycle of its flow. At these moments, one has a chance to be "religious" in James's sense of the word, to enter "a state of mind, known to religious men, but to no others, in which the will to assert ourselves and hold our own has been displaced by a willingness to close our mouths and be as nothing in the floods and waterspouts of God. In this state of mind, what we most dreaded has become the habitation of our safety."[20]

I looked out to the Statue of Liberty again, and back down into the water below. The sun was indeed setting, and I tried to let myself watch it, as Whitman and James hoped we would, for what seemed like many minutes. Just long enough to be glad that I still had the chance.

Acknowledgments

THIS BOOK HAS BEEN a chance—both personally meaningful and hard to face—to revisit a number of themes first addressed in the writing of *American Philosophy: A Love Story*, even and perhaps especially after this love story has come apart. It's been an opportunity to explore, once again, James's insistence that life's worth is up to the liver, and that human beings live most vibrantly in a world of freedom, love, and loss. There are no guiderails or clearly blazed trails. And in the end, maybe this is for the best.

I'd like to thank Kathy for bearing with my sick soul as I tried to finish this book. I would like to thank Douglas Anderson for twenty years of guidance in life and in the study of American philosophy, particularly the philosophy of William James. W. V. O. Quine once commented that Henry Bugbee, his onetime peer at Harvard and the author of *The Inward Morning*, was the "ultimate exemplar of an examined life." I'd want to add Doug to this exemplary list, and am deeply grateful to call him a teacher and friend.

The writing of this book was done as a Miller Scholar at the Santa Fe Institute, with the generous support of Bill Miller and David Krakauer, the president of SFI. I thank Rob Tempio and Matt Rohal for their editorial support and my agent, Markus Hoffmann, for the careful reading that he gave the manuscript at a variety of stages. A handful of editors have helped craft earlier versions of some of these chapters, including Alex Kafka, Peter Catapano, and Sam Dresser.

Notes

PROLOGUE: "A DISGUST FOR LIFE"

1. Ralph Barton Perry, *The Thought and Character of William James* (Atlanta: Vanderbilt University Press, 1935), 1:119.

2. Image discussed at length in Howard Feinstein, *Becoming William James* (Ithaca, NY: Cornell University Press, 1984), 250. Discussed in John Kaag, *American Philosophy: A Love Story* (New York: Farrar, Straus and Giroux, 2016), 32.

3. William James, *The Varieties of Religious Experience* (Boston: Longmans, Green, and Company, 1902), 169.

4. Cited and excerpted from John Kaag, "Madness and Civilization in Cambridge," *The Towner Magazine*, March 10, 2016, http://www.thetowner.com/madness-civilization-harvard/.

5. William James, "The Sentiment of Rationality," in *The Will to Believe and Other Essays in Popular Philosophy* (Cambridge: Cambridge University Press, 2014), 62.

6. Madeline R. Conway and Steven S. Lee, "Alumnus Jumps to His Death from William James Hall," *Harvard Crimson*, February 7, 2014, https://www.thecrimson.com/article/2014/2/6/william-james-grad-death/. Cited and excerpted from Kaag, "Madness and Civilization in Cambridge."

7. William James, *Is Life Worth Living?* (Philadelphia: S. Burns, 1897), 9.

CHAPTER 1: DETERMINISM AND DESPAIR

1. Statistics from "Suicide Statistics," American Foundation for Suicide Prevention, last accessed October 29, 2018, https://afsp.org/about-suicide/suicide-statistics/.

2. Henry James Sr., *The Literary Remains of the Late Henry James*, ed. William James (Boston: Houghton Mifflin Co., 1884), 62.

3. Ibid.

4. Henry James Sr., *A Small Boy and Others*, ed. Peter Collister (Charlottesville: University of Virginia Press, 2011), 173.

5. Ibid., 27.

6. William James, "To Henry James Sr.," *Selected Letters of William James* (New York: Farrar, Straus and Cudahy, 1961), 9.

7. Albert Camus, *The Myth of Sisyphus*, trans. Matthew Ward (New York: Vintage, 1991), 12.

8. *The Blue-Eyed Child of Fortune: The Civil War Letters of Colonel Robert Gould Shaw*, ed. Russell Duncan (Athens: University of Georgia Press, 1992), 29.

9. Ralph Barton Perry, *The Thought and Character of William James* (Atlanta: Vanderbilt University Press, 1996), 203.

10. Louis Menand, *The Metaphysical Club* (New York: Farrar, Straus and Giroux, 2002), xi.

11. William James, *The Moral Equivalent of War and Other Essays* (New York: Harper Row, 1971), 31.

12. Cited in Perry, *Thought and Character of William James*, 67.

13. Cited in Paul Croce, *The Young William James Thinking* (Baltimore: Johns Hopkins University Press, 2018), 50.

14. William James, "To H. G. Wells. September 1, 1906," in *The Letters of William James* (Boston: Atlantic Monthly Press, 1920), 2:260.

15. Arthur Schopenhauer, *Studies in Pessimism*, trans. T. Bailey Saunders (London: Swan Sonnenschein, 1892), 13.

16. James, "To His Father. June 3, 1865," in *Letters of William James*, 1:47.

17. James, "To His Parents. April 21, 1865," in *Letters of William James*, 1:58.

18. For a detailed analysis of James's Stoic background and reading, in addition to this quotation, see Robert Richardson, *William James: In the Maelstrom of American Modernism* (Boston: Houghton Mifflin, 2006), 79.

19. William James, "The Dilemma of Determinism," in *The Will to Believe and Other Essays in Popular Philosophy* (Cambridge: Cambridge University Press, 2014), 117.

20. Josiah Royce, "William James and the Philosophy of Life," in *William James and Other Essays on the Philosophy of Life* (New York: Macmillan, 1911), 12–13.

21. William James, "Huxley's Comparative Anatomy," *The North American Review* 100 (1865): 295. Also discussed at length

in John Kaag, *American Philosophy: A Love Story* (New York: Farrar, Straus and Giroux, 2016), 79.

22. James, "A Letter to His Father. September 5, 1867," in *Letters of William James*, 1:95.

23. Schopenhauer, *Studies in Pessimism*, 25.

24. Friedrich Nietzsche, *Beyond Good and Evil*, trans. Helen Zimmern (New York: Macmillan, 1907), 98.

25. Martin Buber, "The Man of Today and the Jewish Bible," in *The Martin Buber Reader: Essential Writings*, ed. Asher Biemann (New York: Springer, 2002), 57.

26. James, "Dilemma of Determinism," 153.

27. Discussed at length in Louis Menand, "William James and the Case of the Epileptic Patient," *New York Review of Books*, December 17, 1998, https://www.nybooks.com/articles/1998/12/17/william-james-the-case-of-the-epileptic-patient/. William James, *The Varieties of Religious Experience* (Boston: Longmans, Green, and Company, 1902), 160.

28. James, *Varieties of Religious Experience*, 160.

29. Ibid.

30. Ibid.

31. Ibid., 158.

32. Jean-Paul Sartre, *The Diary of Antoine Roquentin*, trans. Lloyd Alexander (London: Lehman, 1949), 17.

33. James, *Varieties of Religious Experience*, 162.

34. Ibid.

35. Ibid., 117.

CHAPTER 2: FREEDOM AND LIFE

1. William James, *The Varieties of Religious Experience* (Boston: Longmans, Green, and Company, 1902), 146.

2. Ibid., 164.

3. Ibid.

4. This quote is often attributed to James, but the source remains unknown.

5. John Muir, *The Athenaeum*, January 18, 1895, 77.

6. Ibid.

7. This passage is discussed often by commentators. Cited in Gerald Myers, *William James: His Life and Thought* (New Haven,

CT: Yale University Press, 1986), 46; John Kaag, *American Philosophy: A Love Story* (New York: Farrar, Straus and Giroux, 2016), 137.

8. Ralph Barton Perry, *The Thought and Character of William James* (Atlanta: Vanderbilt University Press, 1996), 153.

9. Translated and cited in Alexander Gunn, "Renouvier: The Man and His Work," *Philosophy* 7, no. 26 (1932): 185–200, 190.

10. William James, "To H. G. Wells. September 1, 1906," in *The Letters of William James* (Boston: Atlantic Monthly Press, 1920), 1:147.

11. Cited and discussed in Robert Richardson, *William James: In the Maelstrom of American Modernism* (Boston: Houghton Mifflin, 2006), 148.

12. William James, "Renouvier's Contribution to the *La Critique Philosophique* (1873)," in *Essays, Comments and Reviews* (Cambridge, MA: Harvard University Press, 1987), 266.

13. James, "To Henry James Sr.," in *Letters of William James*, 1:169.

14. William James, "My Dear Harry. May 25 1873," in Perry, *Thought and Character*, 342.

15. William and Henry James, "April 1874," in *William and Henry James: Selected Letters*, ed. Ignas K. Skrupskelis and Elizabeth M. Berkeley (Charlottesville: University of Virginia Press, 1997), 95.

16. William James, "The Sentiment of Rationality," in *The Will to Believe and Other Essays in Popular Philosophy* (Cambridge, MA: Harvard University Press, 1979), 77.

17. Friedrich Nietzsche, *The Gay Science*, trans. Josefine Naukhoff (New York: Cambridge University Press, 2001), 6.

18. Cited in Susan Gunter, *Alice in Jamesland* (Lincoln: University of Nebraska Press, 2009), 29.

19. Meaningful context for this correspondence is provided in Richardson, *William James*, 171.

20. Cited in Paul Fisher, *House of Wits: An Intimate Portrait of the James Family* (New York: Holt, 2008), 326.

21. Cited in Linda Simon, *Genuine Reality: A Life of William James* (New York: Harcourt, 1998), 159.

22. Johann Wolfgang von Goethe, *Faust*, trans. John Anster (New York: Dodd, Mead and Company, 1894), 28.

23. James, "The Will to Believe," in *Will to Believe*, 23.

24. Ibid.

25. Thomas Merton, *Love and Living* (New York: Harcourt Books, 1979), 47.

26. Robert Frost, "Notebook 4," in *The Notebooks of Robert Frost*, ed. Robert Faggan (Cambridge, MA: Harvard University Press, 2006), 49.

27. James, "Child to Lowell," in *Letters of William James*, 1:140.

CHAPTER 3: PSYCHOLOGY AND THE HEALTHY MIND

1. William James, "James to Alice," in *The Letters of William James* (Boston: Atlantic Monthly Press, 1920), 1:142.

2. Aristotle, *Nichomachean Ethics*, 1131b.

3. William James, *The Principles of Psychology* (New York: Henry Holt, 1890), 1:104.

4. Ibid., 1:105.

5. Ibid.

6. Cited and discussed in Georg Striedter, *Neurobiology: A Functional Approach* (New York: Oxford University Press, 2016), 80.

7. James, *The Principles of Psychology*, 1:127.

8. Ibid., 1:121.

9. Ibid., 2:110.

10. William James, "The Gospel of Relaxation," in *On Vital Reserves (The Energies of Men)* (New York: Henry Holt, 1899), 50.

11. James, "To Shadworth Hodgeson," in *Letters of William James*, 1:232.

12. Ibid., 1:199.

13. Ibid., 1:200.

14. Ibid., 1:235.

15. David Foster Wallace, *This Is Water* (New York: Little, Brown and Company, 2009), n.p.

16. Cited in Joe Fassler, "Amy Tan's Lonely, 'Pixel-by-Pixel' Writing Method," *Atlantic*, December 2013, https://www.theatlantic.com/entertainment/archive/2013/12/amy-tans-lonely-pixel-by-pixel-writing-method/282215/.

17. James, *Principles of Psychology*, 2:379.

18. Ibid., 1:452.

19. Ibid., 1:462.

20. Ibid.

21. James, "James to Lutoslawski," in *Letters of William James*, 2:175. This point is discussed at length in George Cotkin, *William James: Public Philosopher* (Chicago: University of Illinois Press, 1994), 114.

22. James, *Principles of Psychology*, 2:117.

CHAPTER 4: CONSCIOUSNESS AND TRANSCENDENCE

1. Henry James Sr., *The Literary Remains of the Late Henry James Sr.*, ed. William James (Boston: Houghton Mifflin, 1884), 49.

2. Cited and discussed at length in Linda Simon, *Genuine Reality: A Life of William James* (New York: Harcourt, 1998), 197.

3. William James, *Pragmatism: A New Way for Some Old Ways of Thinking* (New York: Longmans Green and Co., 1910), 299.

4. Colin McGinn, "Can We Solve the Mind-Body Problem?," *Mind* 98, no. 391 (July 1989): 349–66.

5. William James, *The Principles of Psychology* (New York: Henry Holt, 1890), 1:183.

6. Ibid.

7. Ibid., 1:196.

8. Ibid., 1:226.

9. Ralph Waldo Emerson, "Self-Reliance," in *First Series of Essays* (Boston: Houghton Mifflin, 1883), 52.

10. William James, *The Energies of Men* (New York: Moffat and Co., 1911), 14.

11. James, *Principles of Psychology*, 1:230.

12. Ibid., 1:231.

13. Ibid.

14. Cited in Robert Richardson, *William James: In the Maelstrom of American Modernism* (Boston: Houghton Mifflin, 2006), 234.

15. William James, "On a Certain Blindness in Human Beings," cached at the University of Kentucky, last accessed July 9, 2019, https://www.uky.edu/~eushe2/Pajares/jcertain.html.

16. Ibid.

17. William James, *Talks to Teachers and Students* (New York: Henry Holt, 1900), 243.

18. Benjamin Blood, *The Anesthetic Revelation and the Gist of Philosophy* (Amsterdam, NY, 1873), 33.

19. William James, "Review of the Anesthetic Revelation," *Atlantic Monthly*, vol. 34 (1874), 628.

20. Cited in William James, *Essays, Comments and Reviews*, ed. Ignas Skrupskelis (Cambridge, MA: Harvard University Press, 1987), 287.

21. Ibid., 288

22. Karl Ove Knausgaard, *Spring*, trans. Ingvild Burkey (New York: Penguin Books, 2016), 156.

23. James, *Principles of Psychology*, 1:115.

24. Henry Bugbee, *The Inward Morning: A Philosophical Exploration in Journal Form* (Athens: University of Georgia Press, 2011), 43.

25. Ibid.

26. James, "To Henry James," in *Letters of William James*, 2:109.

27. Cited in John Kaag, "Pragmatism and the Lessons of Experience," *Daedalus: The Journal of the American Academy of Arts and Sciences* 138, no. 2 (2010): 63–72, 67; Emerson, "Circles," in *First Series of Essays*, 320.

28. See John Kaag, "Me for the Woods," *Paris Review*, June 30, 2017, https://www.theparisreview.org/blog/2017/06/30/me-for-the-woods/.

29. William James, *Essays in Radical Empiricism* (New York: Longmans Green and Co., 1912), 87.

30. Cited and discussed in Richardson, *William James*, 450.

31. Ralph Waldo Emerson, "Experience," in *Second Series of Essays* (Boston: Houghton Mifflin, 1883), 23.

32. F. Burkhardt, F. Bowers, and I. K. Skrupskelis, *The Works of William James*, vol. 3, *The Principles of Psychology* (Cambridge, MA: Harvard University Press, 1981), 1149.

Chapter 5: Truth and Consequences

1. Josiah Royce, "William James and the Philosophy of Life," in *William James and Other Essays on the Philosophy of Life* (New York: Macmillan, 1911), 18.

2. William James, *The Meaning of Truth* (New York: Longmans Green and Co., 1909), 238.

3. William James, "The Present Dilemma of Philosophy," in *Pragmatism*, in *William James: Writings 1902–1910* (New York: Library of America, 1987), 495.

4. William James, *The Varieties of Religious Experience* (Boston: Longmans, Green, and Company, 1902), 360.

5. James, "Present Dilemma of Philosophy," 496.

6. Ralph Waldo Emerson, "Experience," in *Second Series of Essays* (Boston: Houghton Mifflin, 1883), 66.

7. Ralph Barton Perry, *The Thought and Character of William James* (Atlanta: Vanderbilt University Press, 1996), 279.

8. William James, "The Conception of Truth," in *Essays in Pragmatism* (New York: Simon and Schuster, 1948), 161.

9. Cited and discussed at length in Charlene Haddock Seigfried, *The Radical Reconstruction of Philosophy* (Albany: State University of New York Press, 1990), 260.

10. James, "Conception of Truth," 170.

11. James, *Meaning of Truth*, 39.

12. Ibid., 30–31.

13. Ibid.

14. William James, *Pragmatism: A New Way for Some Old Ways of Thinking* (New York: Longmans Green and Co., 1910), 119.

15. Discussed at length in Alexander Livingston, *Damn Great Empires: William James and the Politics of Pragmatism* (New York: Oxford University Press, 2016).

16. Ralph Waldo Emerson, *Journals and Miscellaneous Notebooks* (Cambridge, MA: Harvard University Press, 1966), 6:197.

17. William James, "The Gospel of Relaxation," in *On Vital Reserves* (New York: Henry Holt, 1899), 48.

18. Ibid.

19. Ibid.

20. Ibid.

21. Ibid., 52.

22. Cited in Gertrude Stein, *Selected Writings of Gertrude Stein* (New York: Vintage, 1966), 75.

23. William James, *Talks to Teachers on Psychology* (Cambridge, MA: Harvard University Press, 1983), 134.

24. Ibid., 230.

25. This point is made in detail by David Foster Wallace, *This Is Water* (New York: Little, Brown and Company, 2009).

26. Arthur Schopenhauer, *Studies in Pessimism*, trans. T. Bailey Saunders (London: Swan Sonnenschein, 1892), 10.

27. James, *Talks to Teachers on Psychology*, 264.

28. Perry, *Thought and Character of William James*, 211.

29. The section discussing James and pedagogy has been excerpted in John Kaag, "The Curse of Credentials," *The Chronicle of Higher Education*, April 6, 2015, https://www.chronicle.com /article/The-Curse-of-Credentials/228999.

30. Ibid.

31. William James, "On a Certain Blindness in Human Beings," cached at the University of Kentucky, last accessed July 9, 2019, https://www.uky.edu/~eushe2/Pajares/jcertain.html.

32. Discussed in Kaag, "Curse of Credentials." William James, "Letter to Henry Bowditch, May 22, 1869," Harvard University Libraries, https://library.harvard.edu/onlineexhibits/james/bottom /2_12.html.

33. Ibid. John Calvin, *Bible Commentaries. Psalms 1–35* (Altenmunster: Jazz Verlag Jurgen Beck, n.d.), 98.

CHAPTER 6: WONDER AND HOPE

1. Cited in Ralph Barton Perry, *The Thought and Character of William James* (Atlanta: Vanderbilt University Press, 1996), 231.

2. Final chapter cited, excerpted, and discussed in John Kaag, "The Greatest Use of Life," *Aeon Magazine*, October 1, 2018, https://aeon.co/essays/is-life-worth-living-the-pragmatic-maybe -of-william-james.

3. William James, *Is Life Worth Living?* (Philadelphia: S. Burns, 1897), 9.

4. Ibid.

5. William James, *The Principles of Psychology* (New York: Henry Holt, 1918), 2:369.

6. Ibid.

7. William James, *The Varieties of Religious Experience* (Boston: Longmans, Green and Company, 1916), 526.

8. Ralph Waldo Emerson, "Circles," in *The Essential Writings of Ralph Waldo Emerson* (New York: Random House, 2006), 252.

9. James, *Principles of Psychology*, 1:329.

10. William James, *Pragmatism: A New Way for Some Old Ways of Thinking* (New York: Longmans Green and Co., 1910), 299.

11. James, *Varieties of Religious Experience*, 44.

12. Cited in George Barnard, *Exploring Unseen Worlds: William James and the Philosophy of Mysticism* (Albany: State University of New York Press, 1997), 52.

13. William James, *Memories and Studies* (New York: Longmans, Green, and Co., 1912), 175.

14. William James, "Letter to James Sully. March 3, 1901," in *The Letters of William James* (Boston: Atlantic Monthly Press, 1920), 2:98.

15. James, *Varieties of Religious Experience*, 66.

16. Novalis, *Novalis: His Life, Thought and Work*, trans. M. J. Hope (Chicago: McClurg and Co., 1891), xviii.

17. Walt Whitman, "Crossing Brooklyn Ferry," in *Leaves of Grass* (New York: Modern Library Printing, 1892; repr., New York: MLP, 2000), 126.

18. James, *Varieties of Religious Experience*, 186.

19. Ibid.

20. Ibid.

Suggested Reading

Primary Literature

The Correspondence of William James. Edited by Ignas K. Skrupskelis and Elizabeth M. Berkeley. 12 vols. Charlottesville: University of Virginia Press, 1992–.

Essays in Philosophy. Edited by Fredrick Burkhardt et al. Cambridge, MA: Harvard University Press, 1978.

The Letters of William James. Edited by Henry James. Boston: Little Brown, 1926.

The Meaning of Truth. New York: Longmans Green and Co., 1909.

A Pluralistic Universe. Cambridge, MA: Harvard University Press, 1977. Originally published in 1909.

Pragmatism. Cambridge, MA: Harvard University Press, 1979. Originally published in 1907.

The Principles of Psychology. Cambridge, MA: Harvard University Press, 1981. Originally published in 1890.

Some Problems of Philosophy. Cambridge, MA: Harvard University Press, 1979. Originally published in 1911.

Talks to Teachers on Psychology and to Students on Some of Life's Ideals. New York: Henry Holt, 1899.

The Varieties of Religious Experience. New York: Longmans, Green, and Company, 1916. Originally published in 1902.

William and Henry James: Selected Letters. Edited by Ignas K. Skrupskelis and Elizabeth M. Berkeley. Charlottesville: University of Virginia Press, 1997.

William James: Writings 1878–1899. Edited by Gerald Myers. New York: Library of America, 1992.

William James: Writings 1902–1910. Edited by Gerald Myers. New York: Library of America, 1987.

The Will to Believe and Other Essays in Popular Philosophy. Cambridge, MA: Harvard University Press, 1979. Originally published in 1897.

The Works of William James. Edited by Fredrick Burkhardt et al. 17 vols. Cambridge, MA: Harvard University Press, 1975–.

SECONDARY LITERATURE

Anderson, Douglas. *Philosophy Americana*. New York: Fordham University Press, 2007.

Barzun, Jacques. *A Stroll with William James*. New York: Harper and Row, 1983.

Bernstein, Richard. *The Pragmatic Turn*. Cambridge: Polity Press, 2010.

Bird, Graham. *William James: The Arguments of the Philosophers*. London: Routledge and Kegan Paul, 1986.

Carrette, Jeremy. *William James's Hidden Religious Imagination: A Universe of Relations*. New York: Routledge, 2013.

Edie, James. *William James and Phenomenology*. Indianapolis: Indiana University Press, 1987.

Feinstein, Howard M. *Becoming William James*. Ithaca, NY: Cornell University Press, 1984.

Gale, Richard M. *The Divided Self of William James*. Cambridge: Cambridge University Press, 1999.

———. *The Philosophy of William James: An Introduction*. Cambridge: Cambridge University Press, 2004.

Goodman, Russell B. *American Philosophy and the Romantic Tradition*. Cambridge: Cambridge University Press, 1990.

———. *Wittgenstein and William James*. Cambridge: Cambridge University Press, 2002.

Jackman, Henry. "William James." In *The Oxford Handbook of American Philosophy*, edited by Cheryl Misak, 60–86. Oxford: Oxford University Press, 2008.

Kaag, John. *American Philosophy: A Love Story*. New York: Farrar, Straus and Giroux, 2016.

Klein, Alexander. "On Hume on Space: Green's Attack, James's Empirical Response." *Journal of the History of Philosophy* 47, no. 3 (2009): 415–49.

Levinson, Henry S. *The Religious Investigations of William James*. Chapel Hill: University of North Carolina Press, 1981.

Marchetti, Sarin. *Ethics and Philosophical Critique in William James*. New York: Palgrave Macmillan, 2015.

Matthiessen, F. O. *The James Family*. New York: Knopf, 1947.

McDermott, John. *Streams of Experience: Reflections on the History and Philosophy of American Culture.* Amherst: University of Massachusetts Press, 1986.

Misak, Cheryl. *The American Pragmatists.* Oxford: Oxford University Press, 2013.

Moore, G. E. "William James's 'Pragmatism.'" In *Philosophical Studies*, 97–146. London: Routledge and Kegan Paul, 1922.

Myers, Gerald. *William James: His Life and Thought.* New Haven, CT: Yale University Press, 1986.

Pawelski, James O. *The Dynamic Individualism of William James.* Albany: State University of New York Press, 2007.

Perry, Ralph Barton. *The Thought and Character of William James.* 2 vols. Boston: Little, Brown, 1935.

Pihlström, Sami. *The Trail of the Human Serpent Is over Everything: Jamesian Perspectives on Mind, World, and Religion.* Lanham, MD: University Press of America, 2008.

Proudfoot, Wayne, ed. *William James and a Science of Religions.* New York: Columbia University Press, 2004.

Proudfoot, Wayne, with Ruth Anna Putnam. "William James's Ideas." In *Realism with a Human Face*, edited by Hilary Putnam, 217–31. Cambridge, MA: Harvard University Press, 1990.

Putnam, Ruth Anna. *The Cambridge Companion to William James.* Cambridge: Cambridge University Press, 1997.

Richardson, Robert D. *William James: In the Maelstrom of American Modernism.* Boston: Houghton Mifflin, 2006.

Russell, Bertrand. "Comments on Pragmatism." In *The Collected Papers of Bertrand Russell*, 6:257–306. London: George Allen and Unwin, 1986.

Seigfried, Charlene Haddock. *William James's Radical Reconstruction of Philosophy.* Albany: State University of New York Press, 1990.

Simon, Linda. *Genuine Reality: A Life of William James.* New York: Harcourt Brace, 1998.

Slater, Michael R. *William James on Ethics and Faith.* Cambridge: Cambridge University Press, 2009.

Sprigge, T. L. S. *James and Bradley: American Truth and British Reality.* Chicago: Open Court, 1993.

Tarver, Erin C., and Shannon Sullivan, eds. *Feminist Interpretations of William James.* University Park: Pennsylvania State University Press, 2015.

Taylor, Eugene. *William James on Consciousness beyond the Fringe.* Princeton, NJ: Princeton University Press, 1996.

Wilshire, Bruce. *William James and Phenomenology: A Study of "The Principles of Psychology."* New York: AMS Press, 1979.

Index

"absolute beginning," 50–51, 55–56

academic career: competition and stress of, 68–69; conflict with Charles Eliot, 164–67; as consuming, 84; James and teaching practice, 148–49, 167–68; loving cup from students as recognition, 161–68; permanent appointment at Harvard, 66; professionalization of teaching, 164–68; scientific research (*see under* science); teaching as vocation, 49–50, 66; writing and publication of *Principles of Psychology,* 66–67

actions: and emotions or feelings, 87; as expression of the true self, 151–52; and formation of habits, 75; habitual, 72, 75, 108–9; instinctive behavior, 72; learning as human activity, 78; meaningful, 108; and neural priming, 75; and "pretending," 63–64; as responsibility, 149–52; self-destructive, 34; will to believe and, 65–66

adaptability: and age, 76; human mind as pliable, 73–74; and Meliorism, 143–44; and pragmatism, 128; stoicism and accommodation to circumstance, 27

advice, well-meaning, 62–65, 87, 138–41

Agassiz, Louis, 17, 23–24

alcohol, 4, 146–47

alienation, 85–86, 107, 156–57; and normalcy, 39–40

Alzheimer's, 116

Amazon expedition with Agassiz, 23–26

ambition, 69–70, 123

"The American Scholar" (Emerson), 7

American Society for Psychical Research, 178

Anderson, Doug, 80–81

The Anesthetic Revelation and the Gist of Philosophy (Blood), 111–15

anhedonia, 42–43; and lack of zest, 153–54; and routine, 70–71

anxiety, 5, 25, 36, 39–40; and freedom, 8

Aristotle, 71–72

beginnings: "coming to" or waking to existence, 118–19; and free will, 60–61, 143–44; free will as "absolute beginning," 50–51; and human relationships, 60–61

belief: and action, 62; as choice, 54; and falling in love, 54–62; in free will as practice of free will, 52–54; love as act of mutual, 61–62; and verification, 52–53, 61–62; as world changing, 5, 59, 62. *See also* religion

Beyond Good and Evil (Nietzsche), 34–35

"bigness," 147–48
Binnenleben (buried life), 149–50
"biofeedback," 87
blindness: habit as sort of,
    108–10; James and bad
    eyesight, 19–20, 25, 33. *See
    also* "On a Certain Blindness"
    (James)
Blood, Benjamin, 111–15, 170
the body: emotions as embodied,
    86–88; mind-body problem,
    98; physical illness and
    existential angst, 38–40;
    physiology and feelings
    or emotions, 87–88; and
    selfhood, 175; and suffering,
    38–44; and transitory existence,
    26, 38–44; and yoga practice,
    88–93, 107
boldness/courage, 60–61, 66, 88
Bowditch, Henry P., 1, 49, 54, 73,
    178–79
Buber, Martin, 35
Bugbee, Henry, 118–20, 185
buried life *(Binnenleben)*, 149–50

Cabot, Ella Lyman, 24
Calvinism, 13, 166–67
Camus, Albert, 18
"Can We Solve the Mind-Body
    Problem?" (McGann), 98
causation, 29–30; and chance,
    36–37; and free will, 51
"A Certain Blindness in Human
    Beings" (James), 153–54,
    156–59, 161–62
chance: determinism as incompat-
    ible with, 36–37; and free will,
    143, 174; habits and minimiza-
    tion of, 81–82; and hope, 174;
    James and personal need for
    risk, 82–83; life as possibly

worth living, 9–10; and "pure
    experience," 115–16; Renouvier
    and free opportunity, 36–37;
    risks and rewards of boldness,
    66; and social inequalities, 56;
    tychism, 47
character: the authentic self or
    "real me," 70–71, 152; as
    determined or fixed, 144; and
    free will, 144; parental
    cultivation of, 14–15; and
    travel, 24
Child, Francis, 67
Chocorua, New Hampshire,
    121–22
choice: and free will, 83; life
    as a, 169–71; and thought,
    107–8; and what one "ought"
    to do, 37
chronic illness, 19–20, 25–26,
    38–39
"Circles" (Emerson), 175–76
Civil War: as context, 18–20
cognitive behavioral therapy, 63
Cohen, Leonard, 116
"coming to," 112–18
compassion, 156–57
"The Conception of Truth"
    (James), 126
consciousness: altered states of,
    111–15; and nature, 119–22;
    and perception of time's "pace,"
    106; plasticity of, 73–74; scope
    and meaning of, 109; as sense
    of existence, 118–19; "stream
    of consciousness," 101–2; as
    subjective experience, 99–100;
    thoughts as personal, subjective
    experience, 101–2; transitions
    of consciousness, 123; and
    transitory nature of experience,
    122; turmoil and heightened

awareness, 115–16; "waking" to, 102–3, 118–20; and the witness, 123

control: circumstances beyond, 2, 11–12, 20, 25–26; and determinism, 12–13, 114; of emotions, 92–93; and free will, 26–27; and habits, 76, 92; James and pursuit of, 68; reason as the "ruling part," 26–27; and "the ruling part," 26–27; and self-determination, 11; and suicide, 34–37

creativity, 4

"Crossing Brooklyn Ferry" (James), 183–85

"Crossing Brooklyn Ferry" (Whitman), 182–84

cummings, e. e., 163

darkness: and mystical experiences, 38, 180–81; and waking, 120

Darwin, Charles, 31, 43

Davidson, Thomas, 56, 84

death: coping with grief, 95–96; suicidal ideation and "control of death," 34–37; survival and psychological resurrection, 46–47

depression: and contemplation of suicide, 18, 170; and existential dread, 38–39; and free will, 93; Jamesian belief as antidote or home remedy, 4–5, 93; and Jamesian "sick soul," 38–41; James's struggle with, 18, 25–26, 38–39, 40, 42–43, 93; and pessimism, 51; privilege, leisure, and comfort as context for, 5, 18; relapse or recurrence of, 51–52; remissions or upturns,

51; as response to reality, 42–43

determinism, 2, 68, 78; and causation (causal determinism), 29–31, 32–33, 37–38; chance as incompatible with, 36–37; and Darwinian evolution, 31–32; "dilemma of determinism," 28; and free will, 2, 12–13, 31, 37–38, 93; human will as special case, 31; James on, 30; and moral relativism, 37–38; and pessimism, 144; pragmatism as protest against, 166–67; and religious doctrine, 12–13, 133–34, 166–67; and Renouvier, 48–49; and "uniformity of nature," 144

Dewey, John, 162

difference, recognition of, 105–6, 109, 146, 157–58, 173–74; and marginalization or exclusion of others, 157

disease: chronic illness, 19–20, 38–39; hospitalization for mental illness, 3; striving for success as, 22–23

The Drummer Boy (Hunt), 18–19

dualism, 28

Du Bois, W.E.B., 163

education: Henry Sr.'s theories of experiential, 14–16; teacher/ student relationships, 148–49, 151–52, 167–68. See also academic career

efficiency, 162–63

Eliot, Charles William, 21, 165–67

"Elysium" (James' home), 6

Emerson, Ralph Waldo, 7, 102, 121, 133, 175

Emerson Hall, Harvard, 7, 164–66
emotions: and activity, 86–89; the authentic self, 83; and the human mind, 53–54; and interiority, 85–86; James-Lange theory of, 87–88; and will, 92–93
"The Emotions" (James), 86, 88–89
ennui, 22–23
epilepsy, 38–39
Essais (Renouvier), 47–49
Evidence as to Man's Place in Nature (Huxley), 31–32
evolution, 31–32
evolutionary theory, 32–33, 43–44
exercise, physical, 79–80
existential angst, 39–40
experience: and assumption of identity and similarity, 105–6; chance and "pure experience," 115–16; "coming to" conscious, 112–18; consciousness as subjective, 99–102; limited nature of human, 132–33; and meaning, 24; meaning as experiential, 109–10; nature and organic possibility, 121–22; "openness" to, 110–11, 121–22; and pragmatic truth, 137–38; "pure experience," 115–18; stream of consciousness and transience of, 103–5; thoughts as personal, subjective, 101–2; as transitory, 122

failure, 65–66, 82
feelings, 84–88, 86–88, 135
financial stress, 69–70
"the fleshpots," 22–23
freedom: and anxiety, 8; and chance, 82–83; Civil War as test

of Pragmatism, 20; and evolutionary theory, 32–33; as fundamental value, 14–15, 19, 55–56, 146; and habit, 76–78; as interest of Alice Howe Gibbens, 55–56; and privilege, 8–9; and social justice, 19, 55–56; understanding limits as, 78–79
free will: as "absolute beginning," 50–51; and activity, 48–49; belief and practice of, 49, 53–54, 59, 93; bootstrapping "will to believe," 59–62, 110–11; and Calvinism, 13; and chance, 36–37; and determinism, 2, 12–13, 31–33, 37–38, 93; and the embodied mind, 54; and emotional control, 92–93; and evolutionary theory, 32–33; and faith, 59; and falling in love, 54–58, 66; and habit, 78–80; and Meliorism, 143–44; neurological basis of, 95–96; and openness, 110–11; and passivity, 56–57; and possibility for the future, 144; practical worth of, 53; pragmatical meaning of, 144; in *Principles of Psychology*, 108; and Renouvier, 47–50; the soul and choice, 28; and stoicism, 28; suicide as assertion of autonomy, 34–36; as unique human attribute, 31–32
Frost, Robert, 66
"The Function of Cognition" (James), 136–37, 142

Gay Science (Nietzsche), 54
Germany, 33
Gifford Lectures, 176

Goethe, 25, 60
"The Gospel of Relaxation"
(James), 149–50
Gray, Asa, 17
grief, 95–96, 116–17

habits, 70–71; activity as habitual,
72, 75, 108–9; and anhedonia,
22–23; as "blindness" of sort,
108–10; and choice, 82; as
conservative, 77–78; and
deadened perceptions, 108–10,
115–16; and flexibility, 74;
formation of, 75; and the
good life, 71–73; and human
flexibility, 73–74; and instinctive behavior, 45–46, 72, 78;
James on equilibrium of, 73–74;
as learned behaviors, 72; and
minimization of chance or
risk, 77–78, 81–82; neurological basis of, 95–96; "pure
experience" and disruption of,
116–18; routine as comfortable,
22–23; self-defeating, 77–78;
and self-help, 71–72; social
transmission of, 77, 80; turmoil
and disruption of, 116–18;
will and transcendence of,
78–80
Hall, G. Stanley, 178
happiness, 88; and security, 68
Harvard: Bugbee's career at,
118–19; Charles Eliot as
president of, 164–67; James's
career at, 52, 54, 66–70, 94–95,
148–52, 159–60, 178–79
Hebb, Donald, 75
Hebb's rule, 75
Heidegger, Martin, 11
Hobbes, Thomas, 18
Hocking, William Ernest, 129,
163

Hodgeson, Shadworth, 81
Holmes, Oliver Wendell, 180
hope, 162–63, 174; Meliorism,
143–44; and pragmatism,
132–33
"hour of rapture," 181
How to Change Your Mind
(Pollan), 115
Hubbard, Elbert, 100
humanism, 163–66
Hume, David, 132
Hunt, William Morris, 16
Huxley, Thomas, 31–33

illness. See disease
illumination, 116
imperialism, 146–47
individualism, 56
individuality, 85–86
instinct: and behavior, 72, 78; for
survival, 45–46
the invisible, 177, 180–81
Inward Morning: A Philosophical
Exploration in Journal Form
(Bugbee), 118–20, 185
Italy, 52

James, Alice Howe Gibbens
(wife): correspondence with,
56–57, 81–82; and falling
in love, 54–57, 60–61; as
intellectual partner, 67; and
marital partnership with James,
66–67, 81–82; and parapsychology, 177–78; as social and
political activist, 55–56; as
source of support and encouragement, 66; "The Will to
Believe" as commentary on
relationship, 59
James, Alice (sister), 14
James, Garth Wilkinson "Wilkie"
(brother), 14, 19, 25

James, Henry, Sr. (father), 34–35,
120; death of, 95–96, 120–21;
and direction of James' career,
16–17; and James' marriage to
Alice Howe Gibbons, 55–56; as
parent, 14–15
James, Henry (brother), 14, 52
James, Herman "Humster"
(son), 96
James, Robertson (brother),
14, 19
*Journal of the Society for
Psychical Research*, 179

Kallen, Horace, 163
Knausgaard, Karl Ove, 117

"The Law of Habit" (James), 75
Leaves of Grass (Whitman),
182–84
leisure, 18
*The Literary Remains of Henry
James* (James), 95–96
"live hypothesis" (as if), 62
Locke, John, 101
loneliness, 36, 85–86, 156–57
love: as act of mutual will, 61–62,
65–66; and coercion or force,
61–62; as long-term habit, 92;
and openness, 110–11; and
zest, 154–56
love letter to Alice Howe Gibbens,
56–57
Lowell, James Russell, 67
Lutoslawski, Wincenty, 91

Marcus Aurelius, 26–27
marriage, 64–65, 83–85, 92, 107,
141–42; relationship between
James and Alice, 55–56, 58,
82–83
materialism, 31–33

"maybe" life is worth living, 9–10
McGinn, Colin, 98
meaning: cultivation of good
character as meaningful
existence, 15; drudgery vs.
meaningful work, 24; as
experiential, 108–10; and
"openness," 118; as personal
and unique, 154–58
melancholy, 11, 42–44, 89; as
horrific, 43–44
Meliorism, 143–45, 168
memory, 116
Menaud, Louis, 20
Merton, Thomas, 65
"The Methods and Snares of
Psychology" (James), 98–99
midlife, 107
mind-body problem, 98
"The Moral Equivalent of War"
(James), 21, 42
morality, 60; ethical communities
and definition of, 157; and
self-accountability, 151–53
Muir, John, 45–46
mysticism, 2, 14, 36, 95, 114,
178, 181–82

Nausea (Sartre), 39–40
Nietzsche, Friedrich, 34–35, 54
Nirvana, 112–13
normalcy, 39–40, 81
Novalis, 181

objectivism, 48
Odlum, Robert, 170
"On a Certain Blindness" (James),
154–59, 161–62, 172
"openness," 117–18; to experience, 110–11, 121–22; and
meaningful existence, 118; and
passivity, 108

optimism: and love, 61–62; and pragmatism, 132–33; as zeitgeist, 42

Origin of Species (Darwin), 31

painting, 16–17

Palmer, George Herbert, 164–65

Peirce, Benjamin, 17

Peirce, Charles Sanders, 47, 121–22

Perry, Ralph Barton, 19–20, 47–48, 134, 169

pessimism, 37–38, 77, 144, 171

"The Ph.D. Octopus" (James), 160–61

philosophy: Civil War as context for James', 20; as lifesaving activity, 3–4; and psychology, 50; as vocation, 50

Philosophy D (course at Harvard), 148–49

physiology: and feelings or emotions, 87–88

Piper, Leonora, 177–78

play, 79–80

Pollan, Michael, 115

possibility: and the future, 104, 144; life as possibly worth living, 9–10; nature and organic possibility, 121–22; and the "twice born," 43–44

poverty, 12

pragmatism, 4, 6, 20, 47; and amelioration, 145–46, 162–63; and amoral relativism, 162–63; Civil War as test of, 20; critiques of, 162–63; and experience, 121–22; free-will's pragmatical meaning, 144; and mystical religious experience, 181; and objectivity, 161–62; as ongoing experiential practice, 170–71;

and optimism, 132–33; pragmatic theory of truth, 128, 132, 136–37, 143, 162–63; as protest against religious determinism, 166–67; vs. relativism, 135–36; and religious experience, 184; and scientific method, 134; and skepticism, 132–33, 162–63; and teaching praxis in Philosophy D, 148–49; as world view and living practice, 127

Pragmatism (James), 129–33, 144, 162–63

the present: "coming to" and awareness of, 114; as transitory, 105; value of the present moment, 122–23

"pretending," 63–64

"priming," 75

The Principles of Psychology (James), 69, 78; contexts of writing, 66–67, 69–70, 81, 93–94, 97; and scientific rigor, 69; will in, 94–95, 108

privilege, 8; and ennui in the fleshpots, 22–23; James and economic and social, 12–13; and suicide, 17–18

Proceedings of the Society for Psychical Research, 179

Protagoras, 161–63, 166

psychology: cognitive behavioral therapy, 63–64 (*see also* habits); James as psychologist, 50, 66 (*see also The Principles of Psychology*); parapsychology as pseudoscience, 178–79; and philosophy, 50, 97; and scientific objectivity, 48, 98–100, 179–80; volition and the embodied mind, 54

"pure experience," 116–18; and
disruption of habit, 115–16;
and risk-taking, 23–25, 115–16

Radical Club of Boston, 55, 56
reason, as the "ruling part,"
26–27
relationships, human, 59–60; as
act of will, 65–66; co-parenting,
92, 139–45; love as act of
mutual will, 60–61, 61–62;
marriage, 55–56, 58, 64–65,
82–85, 92, 107, 141–42; parent/
child, 138–41, 138–45; social
awkwardness, 62–63; social
selfhood, 175–76; stereotypes
of, 140–41; teacher/student,
148–49, 151–52, 167–68; and
trust, 61–62; "The Will to
Believe" as commentary on,
59–60; and "zest," 154
relativism, 135–36, 161, 163
religion: and belief in an
Absolute, 13–14, 114, 159,
177; Calvinism, 13, 166–67;
and determinism, 133–34; and
experience of the sublime,
182–84; faith as act of will, 59;
free will and, 13–14; Gifford
Lectures in natural theology,
176; Henry Sr. and rejection of,
12–14; "hour of rapture"
experience, 181; as out of
touch with reality, 133–34;
spiritual selfhood, 176–77;
Swedenborgian mysticism, 14
Renouvier, Charles, 47–48, 50–52
resurrection, psychological, 44–48
risk-taking: habits and risk
avoidance, 77–78, 81–82; and
sublime experience, 115–16,
182–84; suicide as, 35–36

Robertson, 14
Rose, Steven, 7–9, 171–72
routine: and loss of the authentic
self, 70–71; normalcy and
alienation, 39–40; and
numbing, 71; as survival
mechanism, 71
Royce, Josiah, 31, 127, 129, 147
Russell, Bertrand, 162

Sartre, Jean Paul, 39–40
Schiller, F. C. S., 161
Schopenhauer, Arthur, 23, 34, 41,
157–58, 171
science: anatomy, comparative,
31–32, 49–50, 54, 73; and
causal determinism, 29–33;
cognitive research at Harvard,
95–99; education at Lawrence
Scientific School, 21–22;
evolutionary theory, 31–33; and
"hard problem" of consciousness, 97–99; Henry Sr. and
study of, 12, 17; James and
pursuit of *Scientia,* 17; James as
psychologist, 50, 66 (*see also*
The Principles of Psychology);
medicine as practical scientific
career, 21–22; nitrous oxide
experimentation, 111–15;
parapsychology as pseudoscience, 178–79; physiology, 20,
28, 44, 49–50, 73, 87–88, 165,
179–80; pragmatism and
scientific method, 134; and
principle of sufficient reason,
29–30; psychology and scientific
objectivity, 48, 98–100, 179–80;
and stoicism, 28
seasickness, 42–43
the self: control and self-
determination or autonomy, 11;

and feelings, 85; model of selfhood (material/social/spiritual), 175–76; responsibility to, 149–52; self-destructive behaviors, 33–34, 57–58, 92 (*see also* suicide); "the real me" or authentic, 70–71, 82–83, 151–52; trust in, 64–65, 149–52

self-portrait, James, 3–4

sensations: and consciousness, 100; "hour of rapture" and the invisible, 181; and pragmatic truth, 137–38

"The Sentiment of Rationality" (James), 53–54

"sick souls," 3, 38; and "the buried life" *(Binnenleben)*, 149–52; and disengagement, 58; and life as possibility for the "twice born," 43–44; and self-sabotage, 58; and social privilege, 17–18

"simple ideas," 101

skepticism: and pragmatism, 132–33; skeptical relativism, 161–63

slavery, 19

sleep, 52, 103–4, 154. *See also* waking or "coming to" consciousness

Smith, Huston, 118

social expectations: James as nonconformist, 81; and manhood, 19–20; nonconformism and the authentic self, 150–52

Spinoza, Baruch, 78

Spiritualism, 177–78

Spring (Knausgaard), 117

stagnation, stuckness, 84, 103–4

Stein, Gertrude, 151–52, 163

stereotypes, 140–41

Stoicism, 26–28, 78–79

"stream of consciousness," 101–2, 119–20

"stuckness," 84, 103–4

the sublime, 25, 115, 182

subliminality, 180–81

success: as "bitch goddess," 22–23, 70; James and ambition, 69–70; truth and success of ideas, 136–38

suffering, 43–44

sufficient reason, principle of, 29

suicide, 7–8, 18, 117; contemplation of, 9, 33–35, 85, 170; as cowardice and socially unacceptable, 34; of David Foster Wallace, 107–8; as escape hatch, 35; James as suicidal, 2–3; James' contemplation of, 9–10, 34–36; suicidal crisis and psychological resurrection, 46–47; suicidal ideation as mental illness, 34–35; survivors on attempted, 47

survival of the fittest, 44–45

Swedenborg, Emanuel, 14

Talks to Teachers (James), 149

Tan, Amy, 85

teaching: as competitive and stressful, 68–69; as consuming duty, 84; as human relationship, 148–49, 151–52, 167–68; as vocation, 49–50, 66

temporality: the future possible, 144; and natural experience, 119–20; perception of time's "pace," 106; and transitory nature of experience, 122

Thoreau, Henry David, 102–4, 118–19

thrill-seeking, 23–24
tragedy: and heightened
    awareness, 115–17; of human
    condition, 26, 28, 95–96;
    religious faith as response to,
    133–34
Transcendentalism, 102–3; and
    experiential openness,
    110–11
travel, 15; with Agassiz Amazon
    expedition, 23–26; and James'
    education, 15–16; as recupera-
    tive, 52, 107, 156
truth: and falsehood, 136–37;
    objective certainty and positivist
    theory of, 48; objective truth,
    161–62; pragmatic theory
    of, 128, 132, 136–37, 143,
    162–63

uncertainty, 30, 60–61, 163

Varieties of Religious Experience
    (James), 1, 11, 38–41, 174,
    176–77, 181
via negativa, 153–54

waking or "coming to" conscious-
    ness, 102–3, 118–20
Walden (Thoreau), 102–3, 119
Wallace, David Foster, 85, 103,
    107–8
war, 19–22, 24
Ward, Thomas, 27
"whippets," 111, 113
Whitman, Walt, 182–84
Whittier, John Greenleaf, 55
wilderness: experience of wild
    nature, 119–22
will. *See* free will
William James Hall, Harvard,
    6–8, 171
"The Will to Believe" (James),
    59–62
"The Witness," 123
wokeness, 102–3
wonder, 106, 173–74, 182–84
World Health Organization, 12

Yamasaki, Minoru, 6
yoga, 89–92

"zest," 153–58